FROM THE LINKS

GOLF'S MOST MEMORABLE MOMENTS

JOSHUA SHIFRIN

The Robson Press

To my father, David Shifrin.
Thank you for all your love and support.

First published in Great Britain in 2013 by
Biteback Publishing Ltd
Westminster Tower
3 Albert Embankment
London SE1 7SP

ISBN 978-1-84954-515-0

10 9 8 7 6 5 4 3 2 1

A CIP catalogue record for this book is available from the British Library.

Set in Adobe Caslon Pro
Text design: Sheryl P. Kober
Layout artist: Sue Murray

Printed and bound in Great Britain by
CPI Group (UK) Ltd, Croydon CR0 4YY

CONTENTS

CONTENTS

CONTENTS

CONTENTS

Contents

CONTENTS

Introduction

If you are like me, dear reader, you love golf. From birdies to bogeys, chip shots to doglegs. From a 300-yard tee shot (yeah, right!) to a 3-foot knee-knocker. Is there anything better than pulling out a fairway wood on a par five, gripping and ripping, and then taking that long, glorious walk with just a putter in your hand? And then, after spending a precious few hours making your way through the trials and tribulations of the most worthwhile of endeavors, quaffing a cold one with your weekend-warrior cohorts in the nineteenth hole and discussing the intricacies of the round . . . I just love it all!

Yet, while every die-hard golfer will surely agree that our sport serves up a high like no other, it seems that there is little other common ground. To lay up or go for it? Five iron or three wood? Does the putt break left or right? Yet despite these differences there is one other statement that appears to be universal: that this great love of ours is the most humbling of paramours. Just at the very moment when you think you have it all figured out—*I just need to keep my left arm straighter; keeping my head still is the answer; hit down on the ball. That will do it*—this temperamental lover will pull the rug right from under you and leave you once again completely befuddled, yet somehow begging for more.

It has often been said that misery loves company, and this statement has never been more true than in golf. Every hacker can take solace that even the world's best can fall apart while standing over that little, white, dimpled sphere. And it is this ever-present looming doom that makes their greatness even more spectacular. These incredibly talented men and women, with their livelihood on the line and all the pressure that goes along with it, playing their hearts out in front of, at times, millions of people, have produced some of the most riveting and unforgettable moments in all of sports. Some good moments, some great moments, and some . . . well . . . not-so-great moments. And although Forrest Gump might say, "Golf is like a box of chocolates, you never know what you're gonna get," one thing is for certain: When the question is asked, "What do you get when you put some of the world's greatest golfers under enormous pressure with all of the competitive juices flowing in a battle on the course?" the answer is:

I'd Rather Be Fishing

Ray Ainsley, US Open

The 1938 US Open was held at the prestigious Cherry Hill Golf Club in New Jersey.

Coming into the tournament, the odds-on favorite was the venerable Ralph Guldahl. Guldahl was by most accounts the best golfer of the mid- to late 1930s, and from 1934 through 1939 he put together a total of twelve tour victories. True to form, at the 1938 event, Guldahl stormed back from four shots down on the final round to shoot a sizzling 69 and claim his first of two straight US Opens by six strokes.

Now I know what you're thinking: "Pretty impressive, but is Guldahl's '38 US Open really worthy of inclusion in a compilation of golf's most memorable moments?" You ask a good question. In actuality, the following incredible moment occurred during the seemingly benign second round, and it had nothing to do with Ralph Guldahl, but rather a journeyman golfer and club pro from Ojai, California, by the name of Ray Ainsley. Trying desperately to make the cut, Ainsley hit his approach on the par four sixteenth hole and watched hopefully as the ball sailed toward the pin. Unfortunately, he found the stream just in front of the green, and here's where things got wild. Apparently Ainsley wasn't aware that he could take a penalty by dropping his ball outside of the hazard, so he concluded that he would be forced to hit the ball out of the water.

Ray's problem got worse, however. Bad enough that the ball was in the water, but in addition to that, the stream was moving fairly briskly, and it was taking the ball along with it. So while the ball drifted downstream, Ainsley took one futile hack after another, failing repeatedly to launch it onto dry land, and having to readjust his stance after every miss and then try to anticipate when to swipe at a moving target. As his score continued to balloon, the stubborn golfer stayed the course until his ball eventually, mercifully, found its way onto the green and into the hole. But before all was said and done, the California "professional" posted a *19* on the sixteenth, scoring an almost unbelievable one-hole fifteen over par! Incredibly, this infamous tally has stood the test of time and is still, as of this writing, the highest score ever recorded on an individual hole at The US Open.

After the round Ainsley was able to see the levity in the moment and even commented that he had killed a lot of fish. But when he limped into the clubhouse, the woeful golfer's scorecard tallied up to a jaw-dropping 96!

(PS: In case there was any doubt, our aquatic hero didn't make the cut.)

Am I Seeing Double?

John Hudson, Martini Invitational

They say that lightning never strikes twice in the same place. The following story belies that statement. We're talking about the accomplishment of a relatively obscure fellow by the name of John Hudson who played in the European Tour in the mid-twentieth century. John was born in Wokingham, Berkshire, on August 26, 1945, and he is one of the select few who have been blessed with the talent and determination to reach golf's highest level, having turned pro in 1964. He would play on the European Tour for three years (1971, 1974, and 1976), and while he may not have made the grandiose splash of some of his contemporaries, he was able to eke out a nice living while doing what he loved, playing golf.

The year was 1971. The setting was the Martini Invitational Golf Tournament that was held in Norwich, England. Like this story's leading man, the Martini Invitational seems a rather minor footnote in golf history. But in its heyday the Martini Invitational was considered a respectable event with a list of winners that includes such notables as Greg Norman, Nick Faldo, and Seve Ballesteros, to name a few. The tournament held its inaugural event in 1961 and was hosted by a number of golf clubs in England, Scotland, and Wales, eventually gaining inclusion into the European tour from 1972 until finally closing its doors for good in 1983.

At the Royal Norwich Golf Club, our hero, John Hudson, stepped up to the par three, 195-yard eleventh hole. Hudson addressed his ball, adjusted for the conditions, grabbed his club, and let her fly. The crowd watched as the ball tracked directly toward the pin, and to everyone's amazement, the result was a majestic hole-in-one! As the elated golfer picked his white jewel of perfection out of the eleventh cup, he didn't have much time to celebrate, for there was still work to be done. Hudson made his way to the next hole, the 311-yard par four twelfth, where he once again addressed his ball, once again adjusted for the conditions, once again grabbed his club, and once again let her fly.

What happened next is the stuff of legend . . . a huge drive, a laser-like ball flight, and *another* hole-in-one, this on a par four! Incredibly, Hudson's moment of déjà vu resulted in what is believed to be the only time in the history of the sport that a golfer has aced two consecutive holes in a professional tournament!

John Hudson went on to play on the European Seniors Tour from 1995 to 2000 and is now a teaching professional at the Rivenhall Oaks Golf Club in Witham, Essex. The Martini International is now a defunct tournament and only a distant memory. Yet it was these *two* incredible shots at the Martini that resulted in one of the most unforgettable moments in golf history.

Always Use Your Head
Andy Bean, Canadian Open

Thomas Andrew Bean, widely known as "Andy," was born on March 13, 1953, in LaFayette, Georgia. It could be said that Andy was destined for a future on the links because his father was always associated with the game and even bought a golf course when Andy was fifteen. Andy fulfilled his destiny by taking up the game with a vengeance, eventually winning a spot on the University of Florida golf team, where he was part of a national collegiate championship in 1973, and later inducted into the school's sports hall of fame. And while many athletes struggle to make the transition from college to the professional ranks, Andy Bean had no such difficulty.

As a professional, Bean flourished. He was in the top thirty-five money earners every year from 1977 to 1986 with five top-seven finishes during that span, plus two Ryder Cup memberships to boot. And although he never quite managed to earn that elusive major tournament victory, he can proudly claim three second-place finishes and a healthy stretch inside the top ten world rankings.

One wonders if Bean might still have a fleeting moment of angst about the ones that got away, but it's a good bet that if he does, he'll be mentally replaying the par three fifteenth hole at the 1983 Canadian Open. It was the third round at Glen Abbey's, and after a nice tee shot, Bean missed a very makeable birdie putt, and with the frustration of the day mounting, he clearly wasn't thinking about the official rules of golf. Had he been more focused, he may have recalled Rule 14, which clearly states that the ball must be struck with the *head* of the club. However, as everyone who has ever played our beloved game knows, when you're seeing red on the course it isn't always easy to make the prudent decision.

Obviously exasperated, Andy walked up to the ball, flipped his putter upside down, and tapped in the putt with the grip end of the club. Bean was subsequently informed that the result of this lapse in judgment was a two-stroke penalty, but the real damage wouldn't be realized until the following day's final round, when he came firing out of the gates and carried his momentum all the way through the round to post a record-tying 62. Incredibly, Bean's four-day total of 279 (70, 70, 77, 62) left him just two shots off the lead. That's right, that silly little putter flip cost him a chance at a playoff and a potential Canadian Open championship.

Since turning fifty in 2003, Bean has had renewed success on the Seniors Tour, garnering three titles to date and reportedly enjoying the good life at his home in Florida, where he enjoys hunting and fishing. But in the wee hours, when lying awake with his thoughts, one must wonder if he drifts back to that fateful day in 1983 and contemplates what might have been if he had only used his head.

What Could Have Been

John J. McDermott Jr., US Open

Among golf's exalted names in the early twentieth century was that of a mailman's son born in Philadelphia, Pennsylvania, on August 12, 1891. John J. McDermott Jr. was a good student but dropped out of school to pursue his passion for golf, landing his first job as a club professional at the Merchantville Field Club in Cherry Hill, New Jersey. Reportedly, the young McDermott took every free moment to perfect his craft. He made his way to The US Open in 1909, finishing in forty-ninth place with a rather unimpressive seventy-two-hole score of 322. But John Jr. was not one to be deterred. He kept plugging away, made vast improvements to his game, and just one year later he stunned the golf world by barely missing out on the title, losing in a three-man, eighteen-hole playoff to Alex Smith. Bolstered by his brush with greatness, he focused on the following year's tournament, which would be held at the Chicago Golf Club, and once again found himself in a three-way playoff. But this time McDermott was able to fall back on the experience of the previous year.

The records show that John McDermott defeated George Simpson and Mike Brady in the playoff to capture his first US Open. He was just nineteen years, ten months, and twelve days old at the time, making him the youngest US Open winner to date. Furthermore, the previous sixteen US Open victors had all come from Great Britain, which made McDermott the first American to win his country's most prestigious tournament. The golfing world duly noted McDermott's achievement, but he was not one to sit back on his laurels.

The very next year McDermott not only defended his US Open crown, this time at the Country Club of Buffalo, New York, but in doing so became the first individual to break par over the combined four rounds in a major tournament (currently consisting of The Masters, The PGA Championship, The US Open, and The British Open, aka "The Open Championship"). Although commonplace now because of vastly improved technology in clubs and balls, shooting below par in all four rounds a hundred years ago with primitive equipment was barely short of miraculous. In an amazing display, McDermott shot a combined 294 on the par–seventy-four course for a total of two under par!

Although he was unable to defend his US Open championship in 1913, McDermott managed to secure impressive victories at The Philadelphia Open, The Shawnee Open, and The Western Open, which at the time was the second most prestigious tournament in the United States. With his stunning portfolio in hand, the young McDermott seemed to be destined to become a golf legend. Then, cruel fate arrived unannounced.

After losing to Walter Hagan at The US Open in 1914, McDermott made arrangements to compete in The British Open but showed up to the tournament too late due to complications with his travel arrangements. Then, on the return trip to America, his ship collided with another vessel in the English Channel. Although McDermott was not physically hurt, the psychological effects were devastating. Shortly after returning to the States, he passed out at the Atlantic City Country Club and never recovered mentally. At the tender age of twenty-three, he was forced to retire from the game he loved. McDermott spent most of his life in mental hospitals, rest homes, or under the care of his family.

Although his career was brief, his inspired play is often believed to be one of the reasons that golf became a premier sport in the United States. And though the world had the chance to experience John McDermott's brilliance for only a brief moment in time, golf historian Robert Sommers has sugggested that if not for his mental health difficulties, the Philadelphia-born son of a mailman could have been one of the greatest players in the history of the sport.

No Gimmes

Andrew Kirkaldy, British Open

Like every other serious golfer in the United Kingdom, Andrew Kirkaldy, born in Scotland in 1860, had visions of winning his mother country's championship, The British Open. He took his first crack at engraving his name on the Claret Jug in 1879 and came oh so close, tying for second at the legendary St. Andrews Club. Then, after a seventh-place finish the following year, he didn't play the Open again until 1888, when he tied for sixth.

After several near misses, Kirkaldy must have been champing at the bit in 1889 when he made his way to the Musselburgh Links. Sure enough, he was in contention for the title on the final day of the tournament. As he played the back nine, he knew that every stroke could mean the difference between victory and defeat. So when he played the fourteenth hole and left his ball a mere 1 inch from the cup, he realized that that tiny putt would cost just as much—one stroke—as a booming drive. Perhaps he was miffed that the ball hadn't turned over just one more time, but whatever was on his mind at the time, he took one hand off the putter as he approached the mini shot and casually prepared to tap it in.

And then . . .

He whiffed! Andrew Kirkaldy's putter never touched the ball, thus resulting in a missed 1-inch putt and costing him a crucial stroke on the fourteenth hole of the final round. And as so often happens in sports, this silly, absentminded blunder came back to haunt the Scottish hopeful as he ended the round tied for the lead instead of being the outright champion. And you have probably already guessed the rest. When Willie Park Jr. defeated him in the playoff, Kirkaldy's 1-inch mishap turned into one of the biggest gaffes in the history of golf.

Andrew Kirkaldy would continue to play the Open for years to come. All in all he had fourteen top-ten finishes, six in the top three, and claimed second place on three separate occasions. But his dream of claiming the title would never come true. In the end, after years of top-notch golf, he went out in a fizzle, actually missing the cut in 1910, his last British Open.

Killer Bees

Jack Nicklaus and Gary Player, Zwartkop, South Africa

Mother Nature can turn a round of golf into a disaster. But there had never been anything quite like this episode, which occurred in 1966 in Zwartkop, South Africa, and involved a pair of living legends, Jack "The Golden Bear" Nicklaus and Gary "The Black Knight" Player. Nicklaus, an American from Columbus, Ohio, was born on January 21, 1940, and Player, a South African, was born in Johannesburg on November 1, 1935. Despite their differences in homeland and culture, the two men bonded through a shared regal status in the world of golf, Nicklaus ultimately achieving a record eighteen major victories, and Player amassing an impressive nine majors of his own.

The two future greats were involved in a six-match South African exhibition series. During a practice round in Zwartkop, Nicklaus and Player were with some friends when Nicklaus broke his driver on the sixth hole. This club was the only driver The Golden Bear had ever known as a professional, but he managed to find an acceptable substitute and showed up the next day, ready for competition. The new driver must have proved satisfactory, because the first five holes proved uneventful. But the mystical golfing gods must have been offended by the demise of the Nicklaus driver. Suddenly, on the same hole number six where Nicklaus broke his prized driver the day before, he and Player were attacked by a swarm of killer bees! The two golfers literally ran for their lives and were thankfully left unscathed as they somehow managed to evade their attackers. Then, shaken by their harrowing experience, it took them no time to decide to keep out of harm's way, agreeing to halve the previous hole rather than risk their luck by attempting to replay it.

While Nicklaus and Player are now able to look back and see the humor in their experience, it goes without saying that this situation could have evolved into a serious calamity. While history will scarcely remember that Player got the better of Nicklaus during the six-match display, that infamous hole number six in Zwartkop will be long remembered as the spot where killer bees got the better of them both.

Four in One

Doug Weaver, Mark Weibe, Jerry Pate, Nick Price,
US Open

Even during a terrible round of golf, if a player can manage to strike just one perfect shot, it can keep him or her coming back to the links time and again. And while landing a beautiful chip shot near the hole or sinking a long putt is something to relish, what most golfers fantasize about is the elusive ace, a hole-in-one. Amateurs and pros alike can play their whole lives without experiencing such a magical moment, but as they say, "one can always dream." In terms of hard numbers, however, according to *Golf Digest,* the odds of a professional using say, a seven iron (that's what we writers call foreshadowing) to hit the most coveted of shots is 3,708 to 1! And when the devilishly challenging courses at any US Open are involved, one can only assume that the odds increase tremendously.

Shift to the 1989 US Open at Oak Hill Country Club in Rochester, New York. Thanks to the deluge of rain that preceded the tournament, the second-round greens were mercifully receptive, especially to the tee shots on the par three sixth hole.

The miraculous day started at 8:15 a.m., when a twenty-nine-year-old touring pro by the name of Doug Weaver used a seven iron off the elevated tee to land his ball on a slope approximately 15 feet above the hole.

And then it happened . . . the ball rolled back toward the pin and, you guessed it, a hole-in-one!

Barely more than one hour later, at 9:25 a.m., the thirty-one-year-old Mark Weibe made his way to the 167-yard sixth. Also using his seven iron, Weibe hit an accurate tee shot and the crowd held its breath as his ball landed about 3 feet beyond the hole.

And then it happened again . . . Unbelievably, Weibe's ball spun directly back and *tah-dah!*—the second hole-in-one of the day!

Merely two threesomes later, Jerry Pate, the 1976 US Open champion, surveyed the scene with his club of choice, another seven iron, and at 9:50 a.m. landed his ball in a similar spot to Weibe's ace just moments earlier.

And then it happened yet again . . . but unlike Weibe's ball, which *shot* back toward the hole, Pate's ball slowly drew back and crept into the cup for the third ace of the day.

Finally, Nick Price from Zimbabwe stepped up to the tee with the club *du jour*, a seven iron, and at 10:05 a.m. hit his tee shot on a crest of the green about 20 feet from the pin. As if drawn by a magnet of destiny, the Tour Edition 2 golf ball eased toward its resting place.

And then it happened for a fourth and final time . . . Price's ball found the bottom of the cup, and for those lucky individuals who had staked out the par three sixth on Oak Hills East course, they witnessed an event that will almost certainly never happen again: *four aces, on the same hole, in a major tournament, in under two hours!* And if you think I'm indulging in hyperbole, according to *Golf Magazine,* the odds of any four golfers acing the same hole on the same day are an unimaginable 332,000 to 1!

Tree Hugger
Phil Rodgers, US Open

Phil Rodgers—a San Diego, California, native—was born on April 3, 1938, and grew up to be a golf prodigy with the talent most competitors only dream about. Playing for the University of Houston, he won the collegiate championship in 1958 and turned professional in 1962. At the time, fellow professional Paul Runyan was quoted as saying, "I've never seen a player with more innate ability." Masters Champion Bob Goalby added, "He's got confidence you can't believe."

As Rodgers kicked off the 1962 season at The Los Angeles Open, he was tied for the lead after 54 holes. Then in round four, serving notice to the golfing world, the self-certain rookie shot a nine under par, bogey-free round of 62 to take the tournament by an eye-popping nine strokes. His future appeared limitless; the tour seemed his for the taking.

As valuable as his gifts were, they may have been the very factors that led to Rodgers's undoing at that year's US Open. The site was the venerable Oakmont Country Club, located just a short drive north of the city of Pittsburgh, Pennsylvania.

In the first round, things were going smoothly until Rodgers reached the par four seventeenth hole. It was there that a rare wayward shot found a somewhat unusual lie . . . not on the fairway, not in the rough, not in a sand trap, *not even on the ground!* The ball was resting high and dry in the branches of a fairway spruce!

Unfazed by a situation that would intimidate most mortals, Phil apparently had one of his famous surges of confidence. Rather than taking a drop and accepting the penalty, he opted instead to go for a minor miracle. Rodgers hacked like a lumberjack at the offensive spruce, not once, not twice, not three, but *four* times before liberating the ball, eventually ending the cursed hole with a quadruple bogey eight! A debacle such as this would send most golfers into a tailspin, but such was Rodgers's moxie that he recovered his composure, lifted his game, and over the next three days found himself in the lead at two under par with just six holes to play in the final round.

Victory was in sight. Rodgers needed only a string of ho-hum pars to secure his first major victory, but at this critical point, both his great talent and supreme confidence failed him. Phil bogeyed three of the final six holes, leaving two players you may have heard of, Arnold Palmer and Jack Nicklaus, tied for the lead after seventy-two holes at one under par. Nicklaus would eventually win the tournament in a playoff for his first career tour victory, the prestigious US Open. In retrospect, Rodgers's bravado on a single hole during the first round had cost him a major title. And not only would this fiasco help Nicklaus edge out Rodgers for rookie of the year, but as everyone now knows, The Golden Bear would go on to win a record eighteen major titles whereas Phil would never obtain that elusive signature win.

Yet, Phil Rodgers did not become just a footnote in golf history. He has become a highly sought-after teacher of the game. And as fate would have it, one of Rodgers's first students was none other than his former rival Jack Nicklaus, who credited his teacher with his winning his fourth US Open in 1980 at the ripe old age of forty.

The Babe

Babe Zaharias, Legendary Female Athlete

Nicknamed "Babe" after the legendary Babe Ruth because she hit five home runs in a baseball game as a child, Mildred Ella Didrikson became one of the greatest athletes, male or female, the world has ever seen. Born on June 26, 1911, in Port Arthur, Texas, Mildred was the sixth of seven children in a family of Norwegian descent. Babe was an All-American basketball player, an exceptional diver, a stand-out baseball and softball player, and was even noted to be one of the best roller skaters and bowlers west of the Mississippi. And as if that weren't enough, she also won two gold medals and a silver in track and field during the 1932 Olympic Games in Los Angeles! Yet despite all of these stunning accomplishments, Babe Didrikson became most famous for her talents on the links.

Although she didn't pick up the game of golf until 1935, Babe was, not surprisingly, a natural. Initially she was denied amateur status, so she played her first tournament in January 1935 at The Los Angeles Open, a PGA event. That's right, about six decades before the likes of Suzy Whaley, Annika Sorenstam, and Michelle Wie, Babe was the first woman to play a professional event on the men's tour. Although she shot rounds of 81 and 84 and missed the cut, she proved herself a force to be reckoned with. Then, in 1938, as part of a promoter's gag, Babe was grouped in a charity tournament with two other players, a minister and a professional wrestling villain by the name of George Zaharias. Quite the three-some, but a funny thing happened during that fateful round of golf. Babe and George got along famously, they were married eleven months later, and George eventually quit wrestling to become Babe's manager.

As Babe Zaharias began to immerse herself in golf, she quickly gained a reputation as one of the most talented women ever to swing a club. She earned back her amateur status, and in 1942 went on to win the 1946–1947 US Women's Amateur Golf Championship. She also became the first American to win the British Ladies Amateur Golf Championship in 1947. Later that year, Babe regained her professional status and dominated the professional ranks. By 1950, she had truly hit her stride, winning the Women's Grand Slam by taking The US Open, the Titleholders Championship, and the Western Open, in addition to topping the money list.

Babe appeared in newsreels and celebrity events, and became one of the most recognized sports figures in the entire country. It seemed that she could not be stopped . . . until the unthinkable happened. The year was 1953, and the Babe was struck with colon cancer. Yet, with the interminable spirit that only a true champion knows, Zaharias would not lie down and quit. Babe continued to fight her disease and play the game she loved. Just a month after her cancer surgery, Babe Zaharias made her way to the 1954 US Women's Open Championship. And it wasn't just a token appearance. Despite still recovering from her operation, she took her tenth major championship, and by an astonishing twelve strokes!

This triumph would be the last major victory for one of the greatest golfers of all time. Zaharias's cancer returned in 1955 and, to the deep sadness of her dedicated fans all across the United States, she finally succumbed to the disease on September 27, 1956, at the age of forty-five.

In her amateur career, The Babe won seventeen straight golf events. When you combine those wins with her professional victories, Babe Didrikson Zaharias won an astonishing eighty-two tournaments! Recognizing this golf victory count as well as her prowess in so many other sports, ESPN named her the top female athlete of the twentieth century and the tenth greatest athlete overall. To this day, the name of Babe Zaharias carries a unique cachet that is unrivaled in the world of sports.

Above Par

Jack Nicklaus, Palm Beach, Florida, Charity Event

There are many things to love about our great sport: the drama, the passion, the exquisite timing and athleticism it takes to put a perfect stroke on that little white ball. But for all of golf's finer points, nothing is more impressive than its commitment to charitable endeavors. Although most golf fans notice only the huge paychecks that seemingly grow without end, the professional tour has been doing its part to give back to the less fortunate among us for many years. It actually started in 1938 at the now defunct Palm Beach Invitation, when a then-astonishing $10,000 was donated to charity. And once the ball started rolling, there was no stopping it. In 1987 the tour hit the $100 million mark; years later the total surpassed $500 million; to date the PGA tour has donated approximately $1 billion to a wide variety of charitable organizations across the globe.

Of course it goes without saying that this type of noble endeavor could never succeed if not for the support of its devoted ambassadors. And in this author's estimation, golf has one of the greatest ambassadors any sport could ask for, the legendary Golden Bear, Jack William Nicklaus. Although even the most casual of fans know that Nicklaus is the most prolific major champion in golf history, what is often unrecognized is his incredible commitment to charity. Nicklaus has been doing his part to give back since he turned professional in 1962. And in 2009 the Golf Writers Association of America bestowed on him the Charlie Bartlett Award in recognition of his many years of charitable work with children and their families.

But The Golden Bear outdid himself in a charity event in 1991 when he attempted to break the record for playing on the most golf courses in a single day by a professional golfer. He did so by playing one hole per course as he traversed the landscape of Palm Beach County, Florida, moving as quickly as humanly possible.

Nicklaus continued at his breakneck pace for a frenzied eight hours and forty minutes, and at the end of it all he had played at eighteen different courses. In doing so he not only put himself into the record books yet again but also managed to raise an astonishing $590,000 for charity. And in case you were wondering, his cumulative score was 73 for the eighteen holes, which just happened to be even par. But although every golfer aspires to shoot a score of par or below, on this day the classy Jack Nicklaus was proud to have scored big with his above-par performance.

All in a Day's Work

Mary Bea Porter, Samaritan Turquoise Classic

The 1988 Samaritan Turquoise Classic, played in Phoenix, Arizona, was the site of an extraordinary incident. It involved a professional golfer by the name of Mary Bea Porter, but it was not a feat of golf. Rather, it was an incredibly selfless action, a "Good Samaritan" deed fittingly connected to the "Samaritan" tournament.

Mary Bea Porter was born on December 4, 1949, in Everett, Washington, and was a great athlete who eventually competed in four different sporting arenas at Arizona State University. However, Mary's greatest strengths were on the links, so after graduation she made the decision to try the professional tour, which she joined in 1973. After winning that year's tour-qualifying tournament, she was off and running ... or so she thought. Although she was able to secure a tournament victory in 1975, Porter's golf career eventually settled into mediocrity, and although she valiantly continued to compete, she remained among the rank and file for the rest of her career.

Yet in 1988 Mary Bea Porter achieved something on the golf course that was better than any victory she had ever envisioned. Playing at the Moon Valley Country Club in an attempt to qualify for the weekend's tour event, in the midst of a ho-hum round, Porter's approach shot on the thirteenth hole went wayward and found the gulley near a fence. Porter was assessing her predicament when she glanced over at a nearby home and an alarming scene.

Mary noticed a man dressed in Amish garb holding his unconscious three-year-old son, Jonathan Smucker, by the ankles, upside down, next to a swimming pool, and shaking the gray, limp boy in an attempt to get him to breathe. Mary, who had no CPR training, jumped the high poolside fence with the assistance of her caddie and began to administer mouth-to-mouth resuscitation and pound the child's chest in an attempt to do anything she could to save the youngster. Miraculously, Jonathan came back to life, and forty-five minutes later, with the young boy being rushed to the hospital, Mary hurried to catch up with her threesome, who had continued without her. Somehow she managed to complete the round, and although she failed to qualify for the weekend's event, she was given an exemption to play due to her heroic act. But most importantly, Jonathan Smucker made a full recovery.

Mary Bea Porter is now in her sixties. Her career as a professional golfer may have fallen short of her dreams, but even a major tournament victory would have paled in comparison to her selfless act of saving the life of a child.

A Cool Million!

Greg Norman, The Skins Game

Indian Wells, California, was the site of the annual Skins Game, held from 1983 through 2008 at the end of the official PGA Golf season, and one of the most unusual and lucrative events in golf history. Although the tournament was recognized by the PGA and featured eye-popping prize money that reached $1 million, the earnings didn't count toward the official tour money list. Even so, because the contest featured the tour's brightest stars, and because an obscene amount of money could ride on a single hole, the Skins Game was a crowd favorite and rarely disappointed.

Out of the twenty-six contests, by almost all accounts the most incredible one ever played was not in Indian Wells but rather in the adjacent town of Indio, at the Landmark Golf Club in 2001. Memorable for several reasons, that year's Skins Game included a controversial rule: For a player to cash in on a hole, or win a "skin," he had to back up that win with at least a tie on the following hole.

The four participants for that year were Tiger Woods, Colin Montgomerie, Jesper Parnevik, and Greg Norman, each of them a superstar. When the foursome set out for the day, the formidable Tiger Woods was the clear favorite. But of course anything can happen. As they say, "That's why they play the game."

As the game progressed it was becoming more and more evident that the players were having an extremely difficult time cashing in on the fruits of their labor. Even when one of them scored a rare win on an individual hole, he was unable to at least halve the following hole, thus losing the opportunity to win the skin. As the money continued to roll over, the potential payout grew to astronomical levels, motivating each player to fight tooth and nail to claim the prize.

It was on the sixteenth green when Parnevik sank a 21-foot birdie, placing him in position to win a cool $630,000 dollars if he could either win or tie for the best score on the seventeenth. But Norman wouldn't hear of it. His 10-foot birdie putt found the bottom of the cup to win the hole outright.

Now they came to the eighteenth with a huge payday on the line, and Greg Norman lived up to his moniker of The Great White Shark by halving the hole with a par, thus devouring his opponents to claim the $800,000 skin, the biggest single-hole paycheck in the nineteen-year history of the contest. But then, because the eighteenth was halved, the foursome would go on to a sudden death format. After the first hole left the matter unsettled, Norman struck again by sinking a 4-foot birdie putt on the second playoff hole and netted the final $200,000.

The forty-six-year-old Norman, who had a reputation for failing at the biggest of moments, rebuffed the young lions to stake his claim to the entire $1 million purse. It was the only time this had been done in the history of the Skins Game, and in doing so The Great White Shark put himself into the history books once again.

Bosom Buddies

Hale Irwin, Sea Pines Heritage Classic

The venue for this story is the Sea Pines Heritage Classic in Hilton Head, South Carolina, and the featured pro golfer is the immensely talented and popular Hale Irwin.

Born on June 3, 1945, in Joplin, Missouri, Irwin grew up to be a gifted athlete who attended the University of Colorado. While there, he excelled at golf and football, and in addition to the notable accomplishment of being named an academic All-American football player, he also won the 1967 NCAA Division I individual golf title. The latter accomplishment led to the decision to choose golf as his career, and Irwin turned pro the very next year, a choice that history would prove wise indeed.

In 1971 Irwin won his first of what would be twenty PGA tour victories by capturing the Sea Pines Heritage Classic. Years later he would also be one of only a handful of players to win The US Open on three occasions: 1974, 1979, and 1990. And in the year 2000, Irwin would be named by *Golf Magazine* as the nineteenth greatest golfer of all time.

His record speaks for itself, but the incredible moment chosen for this story would occur at a seemingly routine round of tournament golf. While attempting to win the 1973 Sea Pines Heritage Classic and staking his claim as one of the world's best players, Irwin did what even the greatest of the great have been known to do. He hit an errant shot. And while Irwin was adept at finessing the South Carolina course, this shot landed in a very unusual place ... an article of ladies' underwear!

Irwin's ball had struck a female spectator in the chest and incredibly became lodged in her brassiere. At first the gallery froze, but as it became apparent that the lady in question was not seriously injured, the humor of the situation set in and everyone had a good laugh. Still, as they say, the show must go on, so an official was called in to make a ruling. After some awkward discussion, it was determined that the woman could remove the ball from her bra and Irwin would get a free drop. No doubt even a seasoned pro would have found all of this to be somewhat of a distraction, but Irwin was unfazed. He quickly got back to business and went on to take the tournament by five strokes for his second tour victory.

Hale Irwin would go on to do many amazing things in the great sport of golf, and his efforts would be rewarded with an immortalizing induction into golf's Hall of Fame in 1992. Yet it was a comical mishap way back in 1973 that immortalized the following golf conundrum: Should a golfer always play it where it lies?

Fall from Grace

Tiger Woods,

Disgraced Champion

His proper name is Eldrick Tont Woods, but he's better known as "Tiger." Need I say more? Anywhere golf is played, and even where there's not a golf course within hundreds of miles, it's likely that the mention of the name Tiger Woods will evoke an excited response. Tiger Woods is not only one of the world's greatest golfers but arguably one of the most gifted athletes of all time.

Born on December 30, 1975, in Cypress, California, Tiger was introduced as a toddler to the game of golf by his father, Earl, and his meteoric rise began shortly thereafter on national TV. At the tender age of two (yes, *two!*), he appeared on the Mike Douglas television show where he demonstrated his precocious swing and then proceeded to engage Bob Hope in a putting contest. And from then on the wunderkind just continued to impress. Plowing through any and all competition, in 1994 he capped off an unprecedented junior career by becoming the youngest player at the time to ever win the US Amateur Championship. A stunning accomplishment, but the best was yet to come.

As a professional, Tiger Woods has already established himself as one of the best players of all time. To date he has racked up fourteen major titles, trailing only Jack Nicklaus's mark of eighteen. His seventy-four PGA Tour titles currently ranks second; he has achieved a career grand slam three times over; and he has amassed hundreds of millions through prize money and endorsements. But the world of celebrity has its down side. Sometimes it seems that the only thing a superstar's adoring public enjoys more than building up their heroes is tearing them down ...

In 2009 Tiger appeared to have it all: unprecedented celebrity; incredible wealth; a Swedish model wife and two beautiful children; and the admiration of millions of adoring fans across the globe. And then, on November 27, 2009, at 2:30 a.m., Tiger crashed his Cadillac Escalade into a fire hydrant right outside his home in Isleworth, Florida. Tiger was seen lying next to the car dazed and confused, and reports immediately surfaced that his wife, Elin, had smashed the window of his car with a golf club in an effort to help free him from the wreck. However, as the details began to emerge, it became clear that there was much more to this story. Garish headlines proclaimed that the squeaky-clean Tiger Woods was having affairs with many different women. Eventually confirming the rumors, Tiger subsequently entered a sex addiction treatment center and made a public statement saying that he was "deeply sorry." As his personal life continued to unravel, the humiliated and deeply offended Elin filed for divorce, and several sponsors dropped the icon who only weeks earlier had appeared to be advertising gold.

After an extended layoff from the tour, Tiger finally made his way back to professional golf on April 8, 2010, to compete in the Masters. But to put it bluntly, the young cat had begun to lose his teeth and has only recently started to find his old form. Perhaps worse, he has relinquished his number one world ranking. All of which presents questions that were inconceivable just a short time ago: Will Tiger ever regain his dominance? Will his former legions of fans ever forgive their disgraced idol?

No one knows, of course, but one thing is for certain: Eldrick "Tiger" Woods has had a fall from grace that is unlike any other in the long and storied history of golf. Still, that kind of superhuman talent doesn't just disappear. So a word of caution: Don't poke the sleeping giant, because you never know when he might come out of his slumber to reclaim what once was his alone.

A Family Affair

The Turnesa Family, Band of Golfing Brothers

It is said that golf runs in the blood of those who love the sport. And if one were looking for proof of a "golf gene," one would have to look no further than the golfing Turnesa family. The seven—yes, *seven*—Turnesa brothers of Elmsford, New York, all made names for themselves and their family in the first half of the twentieth century. One might believe that every one of the brothers was born with a golf club in his hand, because they would all grow up to master the game and contribute to its legacy. A few examples:

- Mike Turnesa won six PGA Tour events and most notably finished second to the great Ben Hogan in both the 1942 US Open and the 1948 PGA Championship.

- Jimmy Turnesa won the PGA Championship in 1952 and was a runner-up in the 1942 PGA Championship, falling to Sam Snead.

- Joe Turnesa won an impressive fourteen PGA Tour events and was the runner-up in both the 1926 US Open and the 1927 PGA Championship.

- Phil Turnesa racked up a PGA Tour victory and generally made his living as a club professional.

- Doug and Frank followed Phil's example by also becoming club professionals.

If you've been doing the math, you may have noticed that we've only accounted for six of the seven golfing Turnesa brothers. So what about the youngest brother, Willie? Well, it just so happened that Willie had some golfing talent of his own, but his older brothers wanted more for their youngest sibling. The six of them got together and forbade Willie from turning professional, agreeing to pool their money for his college tuition. And Willie did not disappoint them. He dutifully followed their wishes and made his family proud by graduating from Holy Cross College in 1938.

But though the family had temporarily taken Willie away from golf, they hadn't taken golf away from Willie. Later that same year, the new college graduate entered and won the US Amateur at Oakmont Country Club. And to further prove that teeing it up runs in the family blood, Willie would go on to claim the British Amateur in 1947 and the US Amateur again in 1948.

And in case you were wondering if the bloodline has since run dry, a young man named Mike Turnesa, the grandson of his namesake, just happens to be fighting it out on today's PGA Tour.

Stop and Smell the Roses

Cyril Walker, Los Angeles Open

It seems that athletes in every sport are getting bigger and stronger, and golf is no exception. Strength training and aerobic exercise, once anathema to pro golfers, have become mainstream. But years ago, physical size and prowess were not prerequisites for success. For example, there was Cyril Walker from Manchester, England, who weighed in at a svelte 130 pounds. Born in Manchester on September 18, 1892, the diminutive Walker immigrated to the United States in 1914, and later carved out his place in golf history when he defeated defending champion Bobby Jones by three strokes to secure the 1924 US Open.

Yet despite his accomplishments Walker was known for more than simply playing inspired golf. He was also notorious for playing extremely slowly. We have most likely all experienced the frustration of playing behind a foursome of weekend hackers who take ten practice swings and line up every putt as if their lives depend on it. Well, according to legend, Walker brought slow golf to a whole new level, and during the second round of the 1930 Los Angeles Open, he was in rare form. Besides his usual lethargic shenanigans, Walker was reportedly even picking up imaginary pebbles and cut grass around the ball. Eventually he was warned for slow play at the sixth hole where the brazen golfer retorted, "You won't disqualify me! I'm Cyril Walker, a former US Open Champion! I've come 5,000 miles to play in your diddy-bump tournament and I'll play as slow as I damn well please!"

Finally, as the interminably slow round continued, the tournament officials had had enough. When Walker arrived at the ninth hole, he was an hour behind schedule and he was disqualified for slow play. But Cyril the terrible would not hear of it; he simply dismissed the official's order and continued to play. At this point, the police were called in and literally dragged the irate golfer off the course kicking and screaming. After this melee in Los Angeles, many golfers simply refused to play with Walker, and consequently tournament officials were often forced to let him play alone.

Ultimately, the primrose path that Cyril once walked—albeit slowly—came to a tragic end. The feisty, talented little golfer began to go downhill, eventually succumbing to an alcohol addiction. Financially destitute and out of prospects, he had to take a dishwashing job to eke out a meager living, but that wasn't enough to sustain him. While seeking shelter in a New Jersey jail, Cyril Walker, former US Open champion, died of complications from pleural pneumonia.

Sure Footed

Ernest Jones, Clayton Golf Course

Even if you're fortunate enough to be able-bodied, it's a monumental challenge to master the game of golf. That little ball is just sitting there, waiting to be struck and theoretically posing little or no problem, but we've all seen talented, strapping athletes who have excelled at other sports, stomping off the golf course in utter frustration. Now imagine how much more difficult it would be if you happened to be physically handicapped. Consider, for example, the case of an Englishman who played the game quite well despite a major disadvantage.

Ernest Jones was born near Manchester, England, in 1887. He began playing the game of golf as a youngster, and by the age of eighteen became the assistant golf professional at the Chislehurst Golf Club. Then, he was appointed the club's head professional at the age of twenty-five. His lifelong golfing career awaited him, but just two years later tragedy would strike. While serving with the Sportsman's Battalion of the Royal Fusiliers during World War I, a grenade explosion resulted in the loss of Jones's right leg just below the knee. The prognosis for his career was certainly bleak at that point, but after his return to England, Jones's passion for the game could not be quelled. Driven by an iron determination, he balanced himself on one leg and actually shot a score of 83 at the Royal Norwich Golf course. But the best was yet to come.

In 1920, only five years after his injury, Ernest Jones took on the very difficult Clayton Golf course in England and shot an astonishing score of 72! And while the feat was incredible in and of itself, it was to have ramifications that would reverberate throughout the game of golf for years to come. Up until Jones's incredible accomplishment, the golfing world had assumed that in order to play golf at the highest level, all of the necessary body parts had to function in perfect harmony. Yet, after Jones and others with physical disabilities were able to succeed at playing the game, this notion was dramatically changed. We now know that it is the movement of the club that sends that little white ball flying just so, and though it requires a club head that comes back to square, this can be done without the motion of a perfect body. This seemingly insignificant realization led to a revolution in the way golf is taught and played.

Ernest Jones would eventually receive a prosthetic leg and play on the European Tour. But he also contributed greatly to the world of golf through teaching the sport to others. Ernest would go on to instruct at several of the most revered golf clubs in the United States and work with both amateur and professional students. And in 1977, due in large part to his World War I injury and subsequent golf swing revelations, Ernest Jones would be inducted into the World Golf Teachers Hall of Fame.

Nice Guys Finish Last
Albert Andrew Watrous, PGA Championship

Golf is perhaps the ultimate gentleman's game. In what other activity do competitors call penalties on themselves? Or go out of their way to help their opponents avoid a penalty by helping them find a lost ball? Or follow such formal rules of protocol, such as who tees off first, and treading oh so carefully on the putting green so as not to leave a footprint that might interfere with the other person's putt? Camaraderie and sportsmanship—those are just two of the unwritten essentials. But sometimes such selfless behavior can go too far, as evidenced by the following incident that occurred at the 1932 PGA Championships.

Albert Andrew Watrous, a native of Yonkers, New York, had by most accounts a very respectable career. He was the winner of thirty-four tournaments, played on the 1927 and 1929 Ryder Cup teams, and was a professional at the Oakland Hills Country Club in Bloomfield Hills, Michigan, for thirty-seven years. Despite his list of successes, Watrous never managed to secure that elusive major victory . . . not that he didn't have chances, like the '32 PGA Championship played on the Keller Course in St. Paul, Minnesota.

Back in the '30s, the PGA consisted of match play, and it would be in the round of '32 when an incident of legendary status occurred. As the match unfolded, Watrous was putting a good old-fashioned whoopin' on Bobby Cruickshank and was nine up with only thirteen to play in the 36-hole contest. As the combatants approached the par three sixth green, the outcome seemed inevitable. The dejected Cruickshank conceded Watrous's 3-foot putt and stood forlornly over the tricky 6-footer that he needed to halve the hole.

Cruickshank looked over at Watrous with pouting, puppy-dog eyes and stated, "This is the worst beating I've ever had." The soft-hearted Watrous took pity on the Scotsman. Later, Watrous would say, "I would be going up ten if he missed the putt. Feeling a bit sorry for him and not wanting to see him go down in double figures, I conceded him the putt."

Presumably Watrous had never heard the old adage that states, "No good deed ever goes unpunished." In what seemed like the blink of an eye, Cruickshank went on to win the next three holes and soon had a newfound skip in his step. With the momentum turning, Cruickshank capitalized on the situation and went on to one-putt nine of the next twelve holes. Incredibly, after Cruick-shank sank another long putt on the final hole of regulation, the two men found themselves in a playoff, a scenario that Watrous would have found inconceivable only a couple hours earlier.

As the two men fought through the extended play, neither man would give an inch. They halved the first three playoff holes, and on the 140-yard par three fourth, it appeared that Watrous would escape unscathed. After Cruickshank putted in for a bogey four, Watrous simply needed to two-putt after his brilliant tee shot landed just 2 feet from the hole.

Two feet. A "gimme," right? But Mr. Cruickshank was not as charitably inclined as his playing partner. He didn't concede the 2-footer, and Watrous somehow managed to three-putt from that tiny little distance. Perhaps Waltrous was convinced that fate was against him that day, because when he came to the fifth hole, he choked again. This time it was a 3-foot putt in an attempt to halve the fifth hole. He missed it, and suddenly, improbably, it was over. Bobby Cruickshank had come back from the ashes and pulled off one of the most improbable comebacks in major championship history.

I don't know if the famous baseball manager Leo Durocher ever played golf, but he's famous for a number of sayings, two of which apply here: To paraphrase the first one, "Buy your competitor a steak after the game, but don't even speak to him on the field."

And his most famous of all, *"Nice guys finish last."*

US Open Despair

Sam Snead, US Open

Whenever there's a debate about the most perfect golf swing, the name of Slammin' Sammy Snead is sure to enter the mix. Although his professional headquarters was the Greenbrier Hotel in White Sulphur Springs, West Virginia, Samuel Jackson Snead was actually a native of the state of Virginia. Born on May 27, 1912, in the town of Ashwood, young Sam began his golf career as a caddie at the age of seven, and although self-taught, he would eventually acquire what many have called "the perfect swing."

Slammin' Sammy would go on to become one of the greatest golfers of all time. When his career ended, he held a total of seven major titles in addition to seventy-five more wins, a record eighty-two PGA tour victories. But Snead's career resume had one glaring omission: He never won The US Open. What's more, he is largely considered the greatest player of all time to never have won the United States's golf jewel . . . not that he didn't come close.

Sam finished second at the US Open on four separate occasions; he took third once; he placed fifth twice; and he had a total of twelve top-ten finishes. And a couple of his near misses were heart-wrenching. For example, in 1949, while in an eighteen-hole playoff with Lew Worsham, Snead needed only to convert a 2½-foot putt on the final hole to extend the contest, but he missed the "gimme," handing the title to Worsham on a silver platter.

But of all of the close calls, none was more excruciating than his loss at the 1939 event held at the Spring Hills course in Philadelphia. Going into the seventy-second hole, Snead mistakenly thought he needed a birdie to win the title, when in reality he only needed to make par. Guided by this misinformation, he played the hole more aggressively than necessary. His big drive found the rough and he never recovered, ending up with a triple bogey eight, which placed him in a disappointing tie for fifth place.

Snead's blown golden opportunity for that elusive US Open victory would haunt him for years to come, because with more accurate information he could have played the hole conservatively, and most likely would have secured the one victory that he so desperately desired.

Upset

Jack Fleck and Ben Hogan,
US Open

In 1955 the smart money was on Ben Hogan to win The US Open golf tournament. But a funny thing happened on the way to the final . . .

Jack Fleck was born on November 7, 1921, in Bettendorf, Iowa. The son of poor farmers, Jack played golf on his high school team and caddied for a local dentist to earn some extra spending money. Although he didn't use this money for golf lessons, Jack soon learned that he had a propensity for the game. His talents ultimately led to a position as a golf pro, then a touring schedule, which began in 1939.

After putting his golf on hold to participate in World War II (where he was part of the D-Day invasion), Jack resumed play upon his return. But the soldier from Iowa was unable to find much immediate success. Years later, when he entered the 1955 US Open at the Olympic Club in San Francisco, California, Fleck had yet to win a professional event and wasn't given a ghost of a chance to take the title. On the other hand, Ben Hogan, already established as one of the greatest golfers of all time, was one of the heavy favorites, vying for a fifth US Open victory. But golfers aren't awarded trophies for pre-tournament performances. "That," as they say, "is why they play the game."

Ben Hogan did not disappoint his fans, pulling away from most of the field by posting a four-day total of 287. Most experts assumed that the title would be his once again, as the only man within striking distance was the unheralded Fleck, one stroke behind on the fourteenth hole of the final round. And after a bogey dropped Jack two strokes off the lead, the golf ball that Hogan was using at the time was procured as a Hall of Fame memento. In addition, the television announcers for the event, Lindsay Nelson and Gene Sarazen, actually signed off the air and declared Hogan the unequivocal winner.

Yet someone forgot to tell Jack Fleck that the tournament was over. After a birdie on the sixteenth to close within one shot of the lead, Fleck scored a par on seventeen. He then approached the final hole of the tournament, fully aware that this might be his only chance at glory. So how did he handle the pressure? Simply by knocking in another birdie on eighteen, thus forcing an eighteen-hole playoff.

Despite Fleck's heroics, everyone logically assumed that Hogan would dispatch the upstart underdog. But Fleck was playing with a newfound confidence, and to the amazement of the crowd he held a one-shot lead going into the final playoff hole.

So who would blink first? Well, surprise, it wasn't Fleck! The great Ben Hogan lost his footing as he hit his drive on the final hole, causing the ball to go awry and resulting in a double bogey. Meanwhile, the long-shot Fleck got home in regulation and claimed the only major victory of his career.

The 1955 US Open will be remembered as the legendary Byron Nelson's last ever Open.

It was also the first time the future great, Arnold Palmer, ever made a US Open cut. In years to come, Hogan would go on to win a fifth US Open, and Fleck would only win two more titles on the

PGA Tour. The '55 Open, however, was Fleck's, and it will always be remembered—first and foremost—as the tournament that produced one of the greatest upsets in golf history.

Addendum: Want a trivia question that's sure to win you a drink in the 19th Hole?

How about "Who did Ben Hogan lose to in the 1955 US Open?"

Buffalo Bill

William Earl Casper Jr., US Open

Nicknamed "Buffalo Bill," William Earl Casper Jr. tallied an impressive fifty-one PGA victories throughout his career. Many golf buffs feel he has never been given the respect he deserves, and for good reason. Billy Casper was one of the most prolific tournament winners between the mid-1950s and the mid-1970s, and he has the numbers to prove it.

Born and raised in San Diego, California, Billy started swinging a golf club at the age of five and never looked back. It didn't take long before he reached his potential, and by the time he reached his thirties he was the talk of the golfing world. He was the PGA player of the year in 1966 and 1970, and the PGA tour money leader in 1966 and 1968; he received the Vardon Trophy, awarded to the individual with the lowest scoring average, five times; and he has racked up more Ryder Cup points than any other American player to date. Add that to three major victories and you have the making of a Hall of Famer. But of all Buffalo Bill's notable accomplishments, none compare to his historic comeback at the 1966 US Open.

Arnold Palmer was at the top of his game that year, and at The US Open he was in especially rare form. Going into the final round, he held a three-stroke lead over the field, and after a sizzling 32 on the front nine, Palmer stretched his lead to a seemingly insurmountable seven strokes.

Anyone betting on Arnie was already counting their winnings, but Casper wasn't quite ready to concede as he gained a stroke at the tenth and another on the thirteenth. Still, not a big problem for Palmer. After halving fourteen, Palmer still had an overwhelming five-stroke advantage with just four holes to play. All over but the shouting, right? Nope. Casper promptly gained two more strokes on the fifteenth, two more on the sixteenth, and then scored a par on seventeen while Palmer bogeyed.

They moved to the eighteenth. No blood, dead even. The championship would have to be decided by an additional eighteen holes the next day.

As the playoff got under way, Palmer once again got off to a quick lead, jumping to a two-stroke advantage after nine holes. Then Casper caught fire, outplaying Palmer by six strokes over the final eight. When the last putt fell, the runner-up reached out to shake the victor's hand.

The 1966 US Open Champion? William Earl Casper Jr.!

Billy Casper had a career that was paralleled by few in the sport, but when his celebrated career is mentioned in the laurels of golf history, he will surely be remembered for that stellar performance in 1966 when he crafted one of the greatest comebacks in the history of the US Open.

Comeback

George Duncan, British Open

Now here's a golfing champion whose name few have ever heard before. He was a British chap by the name of Mr. George Duncan from Methick, Arberdeenshire. Born on September 16, 1883, young George emerged from childhood as a carpenter's apprentice, but he also had immense athletic skills. One sport in which he excelled was football (soccer), and he was so proficient at it that he actually turned down a chance to become a professional footballer for the team at Aberdeen. And why did he do so? Because his true love was the game of golf.

In retrospect it turned out to be a good decision, because Duncan had a very successful career on the links. Among his accomplishments were Ryder Cup appearances in 1927, 1929, and 1931, and it was in the '29 event that he both played for and captained the team that claimed the Ryder Cup victory that year. Yet despite this impressive accomplishment, George Duncan is most remembered for his heroics at The British Open in 1920.

The 1920 Championship, which was played for the second and last time at Royal Cinque Ports, Deal, was the first British Open to be played post World War I. Duncan was in the field, but midway through the tournament he wasn't even part of the conversation. In fact, after the first thirty-six holes he had posted a pair of 80s and was a staggering thirteen shots behind the leader, Abe Mitchell.

But day three was a typical blustery one in merry olde England, and it took its toll on Mitchell, who faltered terribly and posted an 84. Duncan was quick to recognize the opportunity, and he set out to take advantage of it.

Aided by a new driver he had picked up at the Championship Exhibition of Golf Equipment that very morning, he shot a stellar 71 to get himself right back into contention. By day three's end, Duncan and Mitchell found themselves tied, two strokes behind the leaders.

Then came day four, and that's when Duncan really showed his mettle. He took charge from the very first hole, shot a solid 72, and finished the tournament with a four-day total of 303. When you consider that he had ballooned up to a count of 160 after day two, and at that point was trailing by an impossible thirteen strokes, it's truly remarkable that he even came near to winning the tournament, let alone coming all the way back to claim victory. In the end he was two strokes ahead of his closest rival, Sandy Herd. It was his first major championship and would turn out to be his only one.

George Duncan went on to become a golf course designer and one of the most sought-after golf teachers of his day, even becoming known as the "the pros' pro." However, his ultimate accomplishment in golf was achieving the seemingly impossible. Like a phoenix rising from the ashes, George Duncan came back from a thirteen-stoke deficit to win the 1920 British Open!

Breaking the Color Barrier
Charlie Sifford, PGA Tour

Until the second half of the twentieth century, people of color were simply not seen on the PGA's hallowed fairways, at least not as players. The protocols and social standards of the time simply wouldn't permit it. But "the times, they were a changin'," starting in baseball with Jackie Robinson, and eventually in other sports such as football and basketball. The barriers in golf, however, were among sports' slowest to come down.

Enter Mr. Charlie Sifford, who was born on June 2, 1922, in Charlotte, North Carolina. In the 1930s, Charlie picked up a job as a caddie in order to make a little extra spending cash . . . with the emphasis on *little*. He was paid 60 cents a day for his work on the links and dutifully turned over 50 cents to his mother. And the remaining 10 cents? Charlie indulged himself by buying cigars, which would become his trademark on the course. He also found a few opportunities to play the game he would grow to love, and was talented enough to shoot par by the time he had turned thirteen. Not surprisingly, the young Sifford had dreams of one day becoming a professional golfer, even though he knew the odds were long. There were a lot of talented players, and the chances of making a living as a professional were slim indeed, even under the best of circumstances. Plus, Sifford's dream had an obstacle in those years that would appear to make his dream an impossibility. Charlie Sifford was black, and at that time there was a staunch "Caucasian Only" rule on the PGA Tour. The bigotry was widespread, but despite the odds Charlie continued to forge ahead and play anywhere and everywhere he could. And he was good. Very good. He went on to win the National Negro Open an incredible five straight times from 1952 to 1956, all the while pushing the golf establishment to open its racist doors. And finally, in 1960, at the age of thirty-nine, Charlie Sifford earned a PGA player card. A year later, with the California attorney general applying immense pressure, the PGA finally relented and dropped their Caucasian Only clause.

In 1967, Sifford finally took his first PGA title when he was victorious at the Greater Hartford Open, and two years later, in 1969, he added to his victory at Hartford with a win at the Los Angeles Open.

Fittingly, in 2004 Charlie Sifford became the first African American to be enshrined in the Golf Hall of Fame. During the ceremony he was introduced by his longtime friend, the legendary South African Gary Player, who eloquently stated, "Tonight we honor a man not just for what he accomplished on the course but for the course he chose in life." And Sifford summed it up best when he stated, "If you try hard enough, anything can happen."

Although racism hasn't entirely disappeared, it now seems unimaginable that just a few short decades ago the likes of Tiger Woods, Vijay Singh, and a host of others would have never been permitted to emerge as international superstars.

What a loss that would have been for the world of golf!

Amateur Greatness
Tiger Woods, Amateur Career

It's an almost laughable understatement to say that Tiger Woods is one of the greatest players to ever pick up a club. Despite his recent trials and tribulations on and off the course, there is a very good chance that when all is said and done, Eldrick Tont "Tiger" Woods will rewrite the record books. *All* the record books. Most majors, most total wins. On and on. And although we normally think of his PGA and Grand Slam greatness, all of it was the sequel to the most stunning amateur career in golf history.

It has been duly noted that little Tiger was a golf prodigy. He had actually developed a legitimate-looking swing as toddler, and he first broke 70 on a regulation golf course when he was just a pup at age twelve. A year later, in 1989, he followed that up by winning his first major national junior tournament. Then, with his momentum growing by leaps and bounds, he made his way to the US Junior Amateur Championship in 1991.

And then it happened . . . Playing a level of golf that belied his years, Woods won the title and by doing so became the youngest winner of the US Junior Amateur Championship at the age of *fifteen*. And then he won again the following year, becoming the first multiple winner of the prestigious event.

And then it happened again . . . In 1993 Tiger pulled off the trifecta by winning the event once again, the only three-time winner to date.

But the best of this unbelievable amateur career was still to come! With the golfing world taking miracles for granted, Tiger entered the US Amateur Championship in 1994.

And then it happened yet again . . . You guessed it, Tiger won the US Amateur Championship, thus becoming the youngest winner in the history of the most important of amateur tournaments. And after repeating the following year, he was in position to pull off the impossible.

And then it happened one last time ... In 1996, at the age of twenty— before he could legally drink alcohol—Tiger took his chances at the Pumpkin Ridge Golf Course in Oregon. In classic Tiger Woods fashion, he made an improbable comeback to once more take the US Amateur Championship. In doing so he became the only golfer in history to win the event three consecutive times. Three junior titles followed by three national amateur championships!

There have been many great golfers in the history of *professional* golf, and history will determine whether Tiger has been the greatest of them all, but when it comes to the *amateur* category, it's hard to imagine that there will ever be a career as impressive as that of the great Tiger Woods!

Breaking Wind

Tommy "Thunder" Bolt, Memphis Open

Given golf's country-club image, there is a widely held impression that most professionals come from privileged backgrounds. But there are many exceptions to this notion, so many, in fact, that the reverse might actually be the case. Consider Slammin' Sammy Snead, Arnold Palmer, Lee Trevino, and a host of others from modest or even deprived circumstances. And although the behavioral norm on the golf course is expected to be gentlemanly, there are some notable exceptions to *that* image, as the following story will illustrate.

Tommy "Thunder" Bolt was born on March 31, 1916, in the remote town of Haworth, Oklahoma. When he was six, Tommy's family moved to Louisiana, where young Thomas learned the game by caddieing at a local golf course. After a stint in the army during World War II, Bolt would eventually join the PGA tour and quickly come to be known as one of the most talented players in the game. In fact he would eventually ride one of the best swings the sport has ever seen to fifteen PGA tour titles between 1950 and 1965, including the champion's trophy at the 1958 US Open. Then, to top it off, after turning fifty Tommy won another twelve titles on the Senior Tour, a resume that anyone could be proud of.

Yet many pundits feel that this was only a fraction of what the immensely talented Bolt could have achieved if not for his Achilles' heel—a horrendous temper! In fact, his short fuse was one of the worst the PGA tour has ever seen. Tommy was known to lose control, repeatedly, which resulted in a multitude of fines and suspensions. He became known as "Terrible Tempered Tommy," and it was his inability to control his emotions that most likely cost him many a title. The legendary Ben Hogan was quoted as saying, "If we could've screwed another head on his shoulders, *Tommy Bolt* could have been the greatest who ever played."

Bolt's reputation as one of the bad boys of golf was widely known, but his conduct at the 1959 Memphis Open shocked even the most seasoned players and spectators. It was a routine day at the event as one of Bolt's playing partners was about to putt, and that's when a loud noise interfered with the poor fellow's concentration.

Was it rolling thunder? Or perhaps an explosion? No, it was Bolt—how does one say this tactfully?—loudly passing gas! This was reported to Bob Rossburg, the players' committee chairman, who stated, "As judge and jury of player behavior, I was obliged to defend the game's honor." Rossburg then confronted Bolt.

Rossburg: "Tom, you and I are good friends, but we've had this report that you farted on the green."

Bolt: "Oh yeah, I just had to do it."

Rossburg: "Tom, you can't do that, not while a man is putting! You're going to be fined!"

Bolt: "Damn it! You guys are trying to take all the color out of the game."

Tommy Bolt was inducted into the Golf Hall of Fame in 2002. He passed away in 2008, but he's also remembered for passing something else. In addition to his prodigious talent, when Tommy's name is mentioned, three things come to mind. One is his great golf; two is his volatile temper; and the other is his colorful behavior at the 1959 Memphis Open.

Hack It Where It Lies

Mrs. J. F. Meehan, Shawnee Invitational for Ladies

Some golfers are more persistent than others. When the ball lands in an impossible hazard, the average guy or gal will take his or her lumps by accepting a penalty and moving on. But there are exceptions. Unwilling to concede a stroke or two, either out of a sense of bravado or just pure, cussed determination, there are those who simply will not shrink from even the most daunting challenge. And just as some golfers are more persistent than others, some challenges are more daunting than others. Way more!

Meet Oklahoma native Mrs. J. F. Meehan, who was a participant in the 1913 Shawnee Invitational for Ladies. When Meehan approached the sixteenth tee box, she chose her club, lined up her shot, adjusted for the conditions, and as the expression goes, "gripped it and ripped it." But reaching the green on the 130-yard par three wasn't as easy as it appeared, as her tee shot landed in the Binniekill River where it proceeded to float downstream. At this point Meehan and her caddie husband had a decision to make. They could take a penalty and re-hit the drive, or somehow try to find the errant shot and play the ball.

Dear reader, you may have already surmised that their choice was not to take the penalty. Far from it. The gritty Mrs. and Mr. Meehan decided they would play it where it lay.

As it turned out, the Meehans were not only avid golfers but also quite resourceful. As the wayward shot made its way downstream,

Mr. Meehan proceeded to commandeer a local rowboat and began following the ball while leaning hard into the oars. Approximately a *mile and a half* later, the ball thankfully came to rest, and after coming that far, Mrs. Meehan wasn't about to turn back empty handed. From her watery stance she began to hack away. One shot, two shots, three . . . forty (40!) shots later she managed to get her ball back to dry land.

But now there was another problem in her way. A dense forest. Hah! No problem!

The undeterred Mrs. Meehan continued her quest, slashing past trees and through branches until she finally made her way onto the green. After the final putt mercifully found the bottom of the cup and the tally was added up, the scorecard for the infamous hole read a whopping 166! A giant number to be sure, but that ornery ball got its comeuppance and ended up in the hole! One can almost picture the perverse satisfaction on our heroine's face as she glared at that silly white sphere sitting where it belonged. No mischievous little golf ball was ever going to get the best of her!

Now that's what I call one for the books . . . or at least this book.

Hot Stuff

Ken Venturi, US Open

Unless you're a baby boomer, or even a bit older, you probably remember Ken Venturi as a TV color commentator with a mellifluous speaking voice and smooth delivery. But before he entered broadcasting, he had a most impressive run as a golf professional whose successful career spanned the 1950s and '60s.

Ken was born on May 15, 1931, in San Francisco, California. He picked up the game at an early age, was trained by the legendary Byron Nelson, and first gained national prominence when he won the California State Amateur Championship in 1951. But Venturi's really big splash came later that year when, still an amateur, he finished second in The Masters by one stroke to Jack Burke Jr.

He repeated as California Amateur champ in 1956, and at the end of that year finally took the leap and turned professional. For the first couple years on the tour he flirted with greatness when he was narrowly beaten by Arnold Palmer in the 1958 and 1960 Masters.

But in 1961 he was involved in a car accident, and although his injuries were not severe, his game began to decline. A stretch of mediocrity continued before his form returned in 1964.

It was during that year that Venturi had several promising finishes and brought his newfound confidence into the US Open at the Congressional Country Club. Through the first two rounds he was in rare form, and in contention for the title. If he could keep his game and his nerve in check during the final thirty-six holes that would be played on Saturday, Venturi would achieve a lifelong dream by winning his country's major championship.

As fate would have it, however, the temperature on that crucial Saturday soared to 100 degrees Fahrenheit, and after several holes Ken began to wilt. By the time he had finished the first eighteen, he could barely stand, but managed to stumble into the clubhouse, where it was determined that he had a dangerously high fever of 106 degrees! The doctors advised him that if he continued to play, he might actually suffer a heat stroke and die on the course! But the headstrong American would not be deterred and literally dragged himself back to the course for the final eighteen holes.

Using salt tablets and ice packs, Ken not only completed the round but actually won the tournament by four strokes! Years later he stated, "I had eighteen salt tablets. Today, you know what they say? That could kill you. Really."

Regrettably, at the end of the 1964 season Venturi was diagnosed with carpal tunnel syndrome, and although several surgeries alleviated the condition, he was never able to find his top-level game again, retiring in 1967 with fourteen career titles. He then would go on to a very successful thirty-five-year career as a golf broadcaster, after which he retired in June 2002.

Ken Venturi was recognized in 1964 as the PGA Player of the Year and *Sports Illustrated*'s Sportsman of the Year. Then, in 1965, he was selected as a member of the Ryder Cup team. But perhaps the highlight of his legacy will be his extraordinary demonstration of will while winning his only major championship, the US Open, and staring down death to achieve it!

No Guts No Glory

Phil Mickelson, The Masters and US Open

Admired by legions of fans for his golfing prowess and winning personality, Phil Mickelson is considered by many to be the most talented player currently on the tour. A Californian native, Phil was born and raised in San Diego and learned the game from his father. Although naturally right-handed himself, he *mirrored* his father's right-handed swing by swinging left-handed. This training produced possibly the greatest left-handed golfer in history. In fact, "Lefty" was an outright golf prodigy from day one. His outsize talent won him a golf scholarship at Arizona State University, and almost immediately he began to rewrite the history books.

As an ASU Sun Devil, Mickelson captured three NCAA collegiate titles and was a four-time first team All-American. In 1990 he was the first left-handed golfer to ever win the US Amateur title, and in 1991 was only the sixth amateur to capture a PGA Tour title when he won the Northern Telecom Open. With this victory Phil was able to turn professional after graduation in 1992. He was not required to go to Qualifying School due to the two-year exemption given to tour winners, and he quickly made the most of his opportunity.

As he started to rack up the tournament victories, the golfing world soon took notice. But as the years passed, these same Phil fanatics were starting to ask when their guy would win a major. As the near misses piled up, Lefty was eventually dubbed as the greatest current player to never win a major.

Then in 2004 his resume was about to change, and in a "major" way. With the pressure mounting on the final Sunday at The Masters, Phil found himself in a nip-and-tuck battle with Ernie Els of South Africa. It came down to the final hole where Mickelson sank an incredible 18-foot putt to take his first major title. And while this was a landmark moment, the real fireworks were yet to come.

The wise among us have long recognized that blessings often come with strings attached. In Mickelson's case, his talent and shot-making ability have tempted him to make decisions that will haunt him for years. For example, the All-American Mickelson had always looked forward to winning his country's national championship.

And in 2006 at Winged Foot he seemed to have his first US Open title in the bag. Going into the seventy-second hole with a one-shot lead, he needed only a par for victory. Clearly the situation called for a conservative approach. A three wood or even a long iron off the tee would surely have kept him in the fairway, but the overly confident Mickelson decided to go with a driver despite the fact that he had only found two of thirteen fairways throughout the round.

And sure enough, his tee shot veered far from the fairway, bounced off a corporate tent, and eventually settled in a patch of trampled-down grass surrounded by trees. Again he went for a shot that defied the odds. This time the ball bounced off a tree. His next shot ended up plugged in a bunker. And from there he failed to get up and down. Double bogey. Goodbye championship.

The fiasco resulted in yet another second-place finish at the US Open, his fifth runner-up performance, tying him for a record. Afterward, a dejected Mickelson summed up his sentiments with a succinct, "I am such an idiot!"

Flash forward to the thirteenth hole of the final round of the 2010 Masters at Augusta, where Phil was once more in contention for the title. His drive missed the fairway and found some pine needles with an ominous tree staring him in the face. Once again Lefty had two choices. He could play the percentages and lay up, or he could roll the dice and go for the green, which stood 209 feet away with a creek looming before the hole. With Winged Foot no doubt in the forefront of his mind, it may have seemed like an obvious decision. But that little man on Mickelson's shoulder was apparently whispering something else in his ear. Instead of laying up, he reached for his six iron and took a monstrous swing at the ball.

While spectators held their breath the ball zipped just left of the tree and then drew right, cleared the creek, and landed a spectacular 3 feet from the hole. The shot is considered to be one of the best to have ever been struck in the history of The Masters. Although Phil missed the eagle putt, he did tap in for birdie, which spurred him on to victory. Soon thereafter he walked off the eighteenth green as the champion for the third time and immediately hugged his wife, Amy, who was battling breast cancer.

After the tournament a reporter asked Phil to describe the difference between a great shot and a smart shot. Mickelson thought for a moment before stating, "I don't know, I mean a great shot is when you pull it off. A smart shot is when you don't have the guts to try it."

Years from now, when Phil Mickelson is old and gray and reflects back on his career, he'll surely have mixed feelings about some of his choices. Yes, he sometimes gambled and lost, at times in spectacular fashion. But good or bad, he's been true to himself. He has dared to be great, and at that he has definitely succeeded.

Not Bad for an Old Man

Sam Snead, Greater Greensboro Open

When it comes to the debate about history's best golfer, two names come immediately to mind: Jack Nicklaus and Tiger Woods. But there's another name from yesteryear that can also qualify for that title: Mr. Sammy Snead. While most fans are well aware that Slammin' Sammy was dominant in his era, what often gets overlooked is his incredible longevity. Snead was among golf's luminaries for the better part of four decades, and he has the statistics to back it up:

- The first PGA Tour player to shoot his age when he posted a sizzling 67 in the second round of the 1979 Quad Cities Open.

- The oldest player to make a cut on the PGA Tour when he did so at the 1979 Manufacturers Hanover Westchester Classic at the age of sixty-seven years, two months, and twenty-one days.

- In 1979, the oldest golfer to make the cut at a major when he did so at the PGA Championships at the age of sixty-seven years, two months, and seven days.

- The only player to secure a top-ten finish in at least one major championship in *five different decades*.

- And until recently he held the record with seventeen PGA Tour victories after age forty, until it was broken at the 2007 Mercedes-Benz Championship by Vijay Singh.

But of all of these impressive "rocking chair" accomplishments, nothing can compare to Sam's incredible moment in 1965. When he entered the 1965 Greater Greensboro Open, he was admittedly on the decline and had not won a PGA event since his victory at the Tournament of Champions four years earlier. But as the greats are known to do, he was able to channel the fountain of youth one more time, maneuvering his way around the Greensboro, North Carolina, course and outplaying men half his age. And despite his age, he showed not the slightest sign of fading.

After sinking the final putt on the seventy-second hole, at the age of fifty-two years, ten months, and eight days, Slammin' Sammy became the oldest player to win a PGA Tour event. In doing so he captured his eighth title at the Greater Greensboro Open, and eight victories at a single PGA Tour event is yet another record!

So while we all acknowledge that Nicklaus and Woods have a lock on the total number of majors, let's not forget to look back a few years before making our final choice regarding golf's greatest player. Slammin' Sammy Snead definitely deserves to be included in the mix.

Snake Bite

Jimmy Stewart, Singapore Open

The Singapore Open was founded in 1961, and over the years this tournament's prestige has grown in parallel with its prize money. Even in these days when megadollars have become commonplace, the Singapore's purse took many by surprise when it grew in 2010 to a staggering $6 million. Aside from the big money, however, there have been some unforgettable moments while the pros were actually fighting it out on the links, and for sheer shock value, one of these moments stands on its own.

The year was 1972, and Jimmy Stewart (the golfer, not the actor) was navigating his way through the course. As Jimmy approached his second shot on the third hole, his mind was surely committed to the task at hand. But then he was in for quite a surprise. A 10-foot cobra slithered its way onto the course and headed directly toward Stewart's ball! Just the thought of this would be enough to frighten the average person, but Jimmy wasn't about to give any ground. Without missing a beat he grabbed his three iron and actually beat the menacing beast to death. At this point Jimmy and the nearby crowd breathed a sigh of relief, but their reprieve was short-lived, because then something happened that was even more shocking.

A smaller, but still potentially lethal, cobra slithered out of the mouth of the larger, dead snake! As the crowd gasped, Stewart once again swung into action (literally) and used his club to kill the second cobra as well!

Although Jimmy didn't win the tournament, and his career will not go down as much more than a footnote in the annals of golf, it's doubtful that any golfer's three iron was ever used for a more serious purpose. Lots of nicknames have been assigned to golf professionals over the years, but perhaps "Cobra Killer" and "The Mongoose" should be reserved for Jimmy Stewart in honor of his kill-or-be-killed action at the 1972 Singapore Open.

The Road Hole

David Ayton, British Open

Here's a name for you: David Ayton. Never heard of him? Well, there's a good reason for that. Read on . . .

As legend has it, when the greatest golfer in Scotland, Allan Robertson, died in 1859, the mantle of the best golfer in Great Britain was up for grabs. Hence The British Open was established in 1860 in an effort to crown a new king. In the event's first year, the tournament consisted of only eight players who battled it out for three rounds at the Prestwick twelve-hole course. Needless to say, Britain's Open Championship was not a very prestigious occasion in those emergent years. But as time progressed, The Open, as it would come to be known, became a tournament that could turn a mere mortal into a golfing god.

Fast-forward to 1885, when the event began to carry some significant clout. Young David Ayton, a native of St. Andrews, was in command as he held a five-stroke advantage with only two holes to play. As Ayton stood over the seventeenth hole (aka "The Road Hole") at the Old Course, the tournament was clearly his for the taking. Despite the fact that this 461-yard dogleg was considered one of the most formidable holes in the world, Ayton was playing at the top of his game with a seemingly insurmountable lead (the keyword being *seemingly*!).

The hole started off well enough. First, a perfectly placed blind tee shot, then a nicely played second shot, positioning David just short of the green. In 1885 The Road Hole was a par five, so he needed only to chip onto the green and two-putt for his par. No problem. In current parlance, *a slam dunk; a sure thing; a no-brainer; it's all good; no worries.*

But what a capricious mistress this game is. Perhaps the kindest description would be to say that David's short game faltered, but to be more descriptive, the wheels fell off. One blundered shot followed another, and the hapless Ayton turned what seemed like a routine par into one of the all-time blowups in the history of major golf. When his ball finally, mercifully, found the bottom of the cup, he had taken nine more strokes to hole the ball, posting an almost unbelievable *11* and losing the title by two strokes.

Alas, such are the fortunes of golf. Over the course of a few minutes, instead of going down in the annals of the game as an Open Champion, David Ayton became just another footnote, one more bewildered victim of The Road Hole.

Sacre Bleu!

Jean Van de Velde, British Open

Although one of the finest golfers ever to come from France, Jean Van de Velde holds a dubious distinction that he would surely like to shed. Born on May 29, 1966, in Mont-de-Marsan, Landes, France, Jean grew into such a talented golfer that he turned pro in 1987 and found modest success a few years later when he won his first title at The Rome Masters in 1993. He continued to compete, and after investing twelve grueling years on tour, he was on the precipice of a life's dream in 1999 when he stood at the seventy-second hole of the oldest major in golf, The British Open, played that year at Carnoustie.

The engraver was undoubtedly preparing to etch the name of Jean Van de Velde on the Claret Jug, for Jean needed only a double bogey to wrap up the championship. Although a French player had not won a major since Arnaud Massey did so in 1907, with all of France behind him Van de Velde stood on the tee with the knowledge that he had birdied the eighteenth hole on his last two rounds and had been playing nearly flawless golf throughout the tournament. Yet perhaps it was this recent good fortune that led to a fatal overconfidence, resulting in what television analyst and two-time US Open champion Curtis Strange called "the biggest sports debacle of all time."

With the golf world ready to anoint him, Van de Velde reached into his bag and pulled out . . . his driver! But why, with a three-shot lead, would he use that club, when an iron would have virtually guaranteed a safe shot? Nevertheless, the undeterred Frenchman stood over his ball and let it fly.

And then, uh-oh, the tee shot sprayed right of the water. Luckily the ball actually found dry land, and Jean still had his grip solidly on the title. All he had to do was lay up and go for the green with his third shot. But that's when he shocked everyone by deciding to roll the dice once again. He went for the green, only to see his ball veer right, hit the grandstand, bounce off a rock in the water, and reverse course 50 yards backward, where it eventually settled in unforgiving, knee-deep rough. From there he attempted to chop out, but his club got caught in that mini jungle, resulting in his ball finding the water it had been skirting the entire hole. And then, in what could almost be classified as a case of temporary insanity, the haggard player actually took off his shoes and socks, rolled up his pants, and waded into the drink. He soon came to his senses, however, and took a drop. His next shot found the greenside bunker.

After blasting out, he needed to sink a 4-footer just to force a three-man playoff, but somehow he managed to keep it together and sink the putt. Too little too late, however. After the mandatory four extra holes, the title finally went to Paul Lawrie of Aberdeen.

Although everyone who watched experienced emotions ranging from outrage to sympathy, Van de Velde was philosophical about the loss, shrugging it off with a comment to the effect that there were far more important things in the world to worry about. Jean continues to compete at the pro level and won his second European title at the Madeira Island Open Caixa Geral de Depositos in 2006. But like other sports figure goats who have snatched defeat from the jaws of victory, the name of Jean Van de Velde immediately conjures up the image of that fiasco at the '99 British Open.

Shark Bite

Greg Norman, The Masters

When the topic of conversation in the nineteenth hole turns to missed opportunities and collapses on the golf course, it doesn't take long for the name of Greg Norman to be uttered. But the head-shaking and tsk-tsks somehow don't carry the usual sense of sympathy that typically accompanies this sort of thing. And why is that? After all, Greg Norman is by all accounts a good guy and well liked among the other pros on the tour. Well, if you want your humble author's opinion, the reason is that the rest of us are just a bit envious. And if there's ever a good reason for the sin of envy, this one might qualify. The man is good-looking, smooth, wildly successful, and one of the best golfers to ever tread a fairway. How can you blame ordinary mortals for taking just a bit of sinister satisfaction from his failures, like when Larry Mize sank that long chip to snatch The Masters from Norman's grasp? Maybe we were happy for Larry, but as for Greg, it wasn't the worst thing in the world for the guy who has everything to get his comeuppance. There's one notable exception to this reaction, however. Read on, and see if you don't agree.

Greg Norman's roots are in Queensland, Australia. And even among the many sports superstars from that island continent, Greg's ascendancy in the sport of golf is nothing short of spectacular. Since turning pro in 1976, he has won twenty PGA tour events, fourteen European tour events, was the PGA tour money leader three times, the PGA player of the year in 1995, and to cap it off has won The British Open twice! Combined with his impressive shock of platinum hair, lean physique, and sculpted profile, he has the entire package and a bank account that rivals the treasury of many small countries.

However, the aptly nicknamed Great White Shark is also notable for his lack of success when it has counted the most. Going into the 1996 Masters, Norman had been a perennial bridesmaid, having finished second on two occasions at The Masters, twice at the US Open, and, you guessed it, two times at the PGA Championships as well. At the '96 Masters, however, it appeared that he was about to shrug this monkey off his back.

As he entered Sunday's round that year, he held a six-stroke lead over his arch rival Nick Faldo. Not only was the Shark playing some of the best golf of his career but Faldo was also in the midst of a personal and professional slump. Faldo had won The Masters in 1989 and 1990 and The British Open in 1987, 1990, and 1992, but coming into this year's Masters, he was suffering from shoulder spasms, had just missed the cut at the preceding Players Championships two weeks earlier, had finished outside the top twenty in all four major championships in 1995, and most painful of all, was coming off an emotionally wrenching divorce.

But Faldo was about to have company in his misery. It's hard to say if it was nerves, bad luck, or just a terrible day at the office, but Norman simply fell apart! After starting the day at thirteen under par he hit one abysmal shot after another; meanwhile, Faldo was turning up the heat by playing a strong round. When the Shark's ball found the water at twelve he actually trailed for the first time, and from there it only got worse as Faldo took command and finished with a birdie on eighteen to notch a five-stroke victory.

Going into Sunday's final round, most pundits were predicting a runaway victory for Norman. Well, they got the "runaway" part right, but it was Faldo who would don his third green jacket at the end of the day. When the final shot had been struck, Faldo turned toward Norman and said, "I don't know what to say. I just want to give you a hug. I feel horrible about what happened. I'm so sorry." And with that both men had tears in their eyes.

Greg Norman is now a very wealthy man. Due to his overall success, he is afforded a life of luxury the likes of which most mere mortals can only dream about. Yet when you mention the name of Greg Norman to most golf fans, it is almost always followed by thoughts of missed opportunities. And none was bigger than the Shark's horrific nightmare at the 1996 Masters.

"What a Stupid I Am"

Roberto De Vicanezo, The Masters

Although the list of South American professional golfers is not a long one, there is one very notable name on that roster—Roberto De Vicanezo. He was a native of Buenos Aires, Argentina, born on April 14, 1923. So prodigious was De Vicanezo's golf talent that he turned professional in 1938 while barely in his mid-teens. Due to his lack of solid mechanics, De Vicenzo used what was often referred to as a "drowsy swing." Nevertheless, he garnered an astonishing total of more than 230 titles worldwide! Among these are five PGA tour victories, three more on the senior tour, and most notably the 1967 British Open.

Yet, De Vicanezo is best remembered for an incredible mishap during the final round of the 1968 Masters, which coincided with his forty-fifth birthday. His performance that day was stunning, starting off with a sizzling 31 on the front nine and then a solid 34 on the back for a final round score of 65. This extraordinary effort should have been rewarded with a spot in an eighteen-hole playoff the following day with the American, Bob Goalby.

It was not to be, however, because De Vicanezo's playing partner, Tommy Aaron, inadvertently marked Roberto's playing card with a 4 although he had actually posted a birdie 3 on the seventeenth hole. Unfortunately the mistake went unnoticed, so after Roberto signed the card and formally submitted it, the strict rules of golf stipulated that the higher score would stand. As a result there was no playoff, and Roberto, the hapless victim, was deemed the runner-up, handing the title to Goalby. The fair-minded Goalby was reluctant to accept it, but the rules were the rules and there was no appeal. In a subsequent interview, the classy De Vicanezo declined to blame Tommy Aaron for his error, instead blaming himself for failing to carefully check his scorecard, and uttering what is now his legendary quote: "What a stupid I am!"

Roberto was inducted into Golf's Hall of Fame in 1989 and officially retired from the game on November 12, 2006, at the age of eighty-three. Yet despite a career studded with one highlight accomplishment after another, the likeable and popular Argentinian will always be remembered for one of the most costly oversights in the history of the Masters and for his poignant statement that summed it all up: "What a stupid I am!"

Ants in My Pants

Jack Newton, Cock O' the North Tournament

"Down Under" is often associated with Greg Norman, but he's not the only golf celebrity from the island nation of Australia. Perhaps you haven't heard of him, but Jack Newton is also an Aussie who could play the game, and quite proficiently. Newton was born on January 30, 1950, in Cessnock, New South Wales, and like many others in this book, he had a golfing talent that was rivaled only by his love for the sport. After honing his craft during his formative years, the twenty-one-year-old Newton turned professional in 1971 and quickly found success. Just one year later he won his first tournament at The Dutch Open and ultimately became one of Australia's most prolific golfers of the 1970s and early 1980s. He racked up thirteen victories during his time as a professional and is often remembered for his heartbreaking playoff loss to Tom Watson at the 1975 British Open.

But in 1975, Jack had an experience at the little-known Cock o' the North Tournament in Ndola, Zambia, which he's not likely to ever forget. As the tournament progressed, Newton was in contention for the title when he approached the seventeenth hole. That's when the unsuspecting Aussie's ball landed next to a nest of African ants, and before he could say "holy bloke," he was attacked by the ferocious little devils. As he was repeatedly bitten, the terrified Newton quite literally tore off his clothes and subsequently ran off the course.

Later, Newton was somehow able to regain his composure and return to the course to complete his round. Then the very next day he couldn't believe his eyes when he noticed an attractive female spectator suffering the same fate. After the gorgeous woman tore off her clothes and ran off the course, it took all of Jack's concentration to focus on the task at hand. Yet he managed not only to keep his composure but also actually go on to win the tournament!

Jack Newton would go on to win the PGA Tour of Australia's Order of Merit in 1979 and would finish tied for second at the 1980 Masters. Unfortunately, on July 24, 1983, while his career was at its pinnacle, he had a near-fatal accident when he was struck by the propeller of a Cessna airplane. As a result of this horrendous incident, Newton lost his right arm and eye and also sustained abdominal injuries. Thankfully he survived, but of course his professional playing days were over. Jack's love for golf never wavered, however. In a feat of incredible willpower, he learned to play one-handed and typically scores in the mid-80s.

Jack Newton had a golf career that, although tragically cut short, left him with a lifetime full of memories. But of all his experiences, it was a freak mishap with a nest full of angry ants that led to one of the wackiest moments in tournament golf history.

The Greatest Tournament Ever Played
Francis DeSales Ouimet, US Open

May 8, 1893, was the auspicious day that saw the birth of future legend Francis DeSales Ouimet. The Ouimet family lived in Brookline, Massachusetts, but his was the first generation of Ouimets born in America. His father, Arthur, was French-Canadian, and his mother, Mary, was a native of Ireland. Not surprisingly, given the times, the immigrant Ouimet family was struggling financially and had difficulty making ends meet. Yet as fate would have it, when young Francis was four years old, the family somehow managed to purchase a home across from the seventeenth hole of "The Country Club" and that set the stage for golfing history.

To help supplement his family's income, Francis began to caddie at the age of eleven and soon fell in love with the game. Equipped with only one golf club, which he borrowed from his brother, Ouimet taught himself the game of golf, and his natural talent and passion for the sport propelled him through the ranks.

Francis continued to hone his skills and found his first large taste of success when he won the Massachusetts Amateur title in 1913 at the age of twenty. In response to this prestigious victory, the president of the United States Golf Association, Robert Watson, personally asked Francis to participate in The US Open. But despite the once-in-a-lifetime opportunity, Ouimet originally decided to forgo the event as it interfered with his work schedule. However, when his employer granted him a short leave of absence, Ouimet was off to make history.

As the event got under way, he managed to hold his nerve, and after a round or two, to the surprise of many the longshot Ouimet actually found himself flirting with the top of the leader board. He then shocked the golf world by finishing the regulation four rounds in a three-way tie with the four-time British Open winner Harry Vardon and the reigning British Open Champion, Ted Ray. Even though he shared the lead, few gave the unheralded Ouimet even a slim chance of hanging with the big boys on the final day.

As the playoff unfolded, the front nine ended with all three men tied at 38, so the title came down to the final nine holes. At this point the crowd began to buzz. Could Ouimet continue to hold his nerve? Could this upstart from a meager background turn the golf world on its ear?

The answer was triumphant. When Vardon and Ray both three-putted the par three tenth, Ouimet jumped out in front. And as the playoff wore on, it was Ray who blinked first and fell well off the pace. On the seventeenth, with Vardon only one shot behind Ouimet's tenuous lead, the Brit caught a bunker with his drive and had to settle for bogey. Suddenly the title was the underdog Ouimet's for the taking, and he was up to the task. While the astonished spectators watched, he sank a 15-foot birdie and moments later was declared the victor.

In one of the biggest upsets in the history of the sport, Francis Ouimet, the son of a poor immigrant family, claimed his country's most heralded golf title. Those who witnessed that day's events knew that golfing history had been made, and that the repercussions would continue to be felt for years to come.

In 1913 it was estimated that there were about 350,000 American golfers. This was about to change, and how! Ouimet's stunning win made headlines across the nation, and just a decade after one of the most amazing victories in the sport's history, two million were playing the game. By most accounts this near sixfold increase was in direct response to Ouimet's instant fame.

Ouimet would go on to win the US Amateur title on two separate occasions (1914 and 1931). He also played on the first eight Walker Cup Teams and would later become its captain. In 1951 Ouimet had the distinction of becoming the first American to be named the Captain of the Royal and Ancient Golf Club of St. Andrews. And for the *coup de gras*, in 1974 Ouimet was inducted posthumously into golf's hallowed Hall of Fame.

Francis DeSales Ouimet passed away on September 2, 1967. In his seventy-four years the one-time caddie from Brookline, Massachusetts, had a lifetime of amazing accomplishments. But the beloved little scrapper will be remembered first and foremost for his legendary heroics in the 1913 US Open and its subsequent transformation of the game we love . . . the great game of golf!

Southpaw

Wilber Artist Stackhouse, Outlandish Antics

Sometimes this game just isn't fair. You can be playing the round of your life when, out of nowhere, a couple wayward shots pop up and your chance to break 80 disappears in a puff. It's enough to turn even a pacifist into a raging lunatic. And it doesn't only happen to amateurs. Even the pros have been known to curse uncontrollably, engage in nasty verbal exchanges with fans, break clubs over their knees, argue vehemently with officials, and pull their hair or fall to the ground in frustration. But perhaps the champion of erratic behavior is a volatile Texan by the name of Wilber Artist Stackhouse, who went by the handle of "Lefty" long before Phil Mickelson appeared on the scene.

Lefty Stackhouse, an outlandish cuss with leathery skin and a hardened personality to match, was one of the best professional golfers of the 1930s and 1940s. Yet Lefty had an Achilles' heel in the form of a hot temper. And the term "hot" just might be the quintessential understatement. After a poor shot Lefty was not one to simply yell, curse, or angrily swipe his club. To Lefty that was mere child's play. If he determined that he had made a poor effort, he would literally punish the part of his body that he held responsible for the inadequacy.

Let me explain. On one occasion, after Lefty hooked a drive, which he was known to do, he shoved his arm into a thorny rosebush, leaving his mutilated appendage a bloody mess. If he deemed that he had misread a putt, he would bang his head against his putter, a tree,

81

a rock, or whatever else he felt would inflict a suitable punishment. And in one of his most famous explosions of anger, Lefty threw his clubs and bag into a water hazard ... and then he picked up his caddie and threw him in as well!

But of all Lefty Stackhouse's angry antics, his most outrageous was best described by former professional and television analyst Ken Venturi. As Venturi eloquently stated, "One time when he missed a short putt, Lefty punched himself right in the jaw with an uppercut. He hit himself so hard he fell to his knees. Then he hit himself again and knocked himself out!" Yes, that really happened. Lefty Stackhouse literally beat himself unconscious in the middle of his round!

In a fit of pique, professional athletes have done some astounding things, but perhaps none quite as extraordinary as knocking themselves unconscious. This is the sort of thing that can leave one at a loss for words, but I guess you could say that whenever Lefty Stackhouse entered a tournament, he always had at least a puncher's chance.

What Goes Up Must Come Down
Robert Allan Cruickshank, US Open

Robert Allan Cruickshank, known simply as "Bobby," was born on November 16, 1894, in Grantown-on-Spey, Scotland. The Scot had a personality much larger than his 5-foot, 5-inch (1.65-meter) stature. Cruickshank's talent and passion led to a professional career in 1921, and soon thereafter the charismatic little guy made his way across the pond to the United States, where he was practically adopted by the Americans. The feeling appeared to be mutual, too, as Bobby found immediate success by reaching the PGA semifinals in 1922 and then again in 1923. Although he would succumb on both occasions to eventual champion Gene Sarazen, Cruickshank must have been bolstered by his brush with a major victory. In 1923 there would be more near misses, including a shot at immortality at that year's US Open, but with a finish as the runner-up. As the years passed and Cruickshank continued to fall short of his dream of a major championship, finishing second again at The US Open in 1932, one must have wondered if the man was losing hope.

Finally, at the 1934 US Open, Cruickshank was so close to that elusive major title that he must have been able to taste it. He held the lead on the final day with only eight holes left to play. Then, on the eleventh hole, his shot went awry and headed directly toward a creek. Miraculously, the golfing gods smiled on Cruickshank as his ball skipped over the water, hit a rock, and amazingly ended up directly on the putting green! The thrilled Cruickshank was ecstatic and threw his club high into the air in celebration. But alas, the golfing gods are a finicky bunch, and they quickly turned their backs on Bobby. The club came down directly on his head, knocking him completely unconscious. Thankfully he was revived and gallantly continued to play, but not surprisingly he was still somewhat woozy. He failed to play his best, and when the shots were eventually tallied, Cruickshank was a bridesmaid yet again, finishing in a tie for third.

Bobby Cruickshank would win seventeen tour events throughout his career but never would capture that long-sought-after major title. Perhaps if he had been more of a science scholar, he might have thought twice before launching that ill-fated golf club into the air, and history might well have told a different tale. For as every first-year physics student can tell you, "What goes up must come down."

Plus Fours

Payne Stewart, US Open

William Payne Stewart was born on January 30, 1957, in Springfield, Missouri. Growing up in the Midwest, young Payne was instructed on the finer points of the game by his father, who had his own credentials, having played in the 1955 US Open. Payne had a stellar junior career and eventually played his collegiate golf at Southern Methodist University. Following his college career, he turned professional in 1979. Initially it wasn't a bed of roses. Stewart failed to make it through Qualifying School and was relegated to the Asian Tour. While playing in the Far East may not have been Stewart's ideal venue, he made the most of the opportunity, winning twice. And just two years later, Payne's dream came true as he played his way onto the PGA Tour.

Stewart quickly became a crowd favorite in large part due to his fashion sense. Beginning in 1982, he began to wear flat-billed hats and "plus fours," so named because they are shortened pants that extend 4 inches below the knee. Worn with colorful stockings, this outfit met with enthusiastic fan approval and quickly became Payne's trademark look. He was bringing some pizzazz to the game and finding some success early in his career, but he was often criticized for not living up to his talent. After coming up just short in three majors in 1985–86, he had to endure the skeptics who seemed to be growing by the day. He would eventually silence his naysayers by capturing his first major at the 1989 PGA Championship, and two years later the patriotic American would win his country's crown jewel by securing the 1991 US Open.

His Open win was followed by a long dry spell, however. After nearly a decade without another major victory, Stewart felt the desperate hunger of a starving man as he entered the 1999 US Open on the legendary Course Number Two in Pinehurst, North Carolina.

The US Open is notorious for featuring some of the most difficult conditions in the game. Facing narrow fairways, deep roughs, and lightning-fast greens, a golfer must be at his best mentally and physically to conquer the beast. As a former champion, Stewart remembered the taste of victory, and he began by rising to the occasion, finishing the first round at two under par, just one shot off the lead. On day two his combined score was 137, sharing the lead at three under par. Day three saw him post a two above par, but the course must have been playing harder that day, because when that round was over Payne sat atop the leader board, tenaciously holding on to a one-shot advantage. If he could hold his nerve he was only twenty-four hours away from becoming a two-time US Open champion.

As he teed off on the last round, Payne was paired with fellow American Phil Mickelson, and the two compatriots engaged in a classic duel. The match was tight all the way, and after Stewart took a one-shot advantage with a birdie on seventeen, he was only one hole away from pay dirt. But there are never any easy holes at The US Open. On number eighteen, Payne's tee shot went wayward, making his job all the more difficult. He did eventually get to the green, but his putt for par was a daunting 15 feet from the hole. If he missed and scored a bogey, a playoff would ensue.

While the breathless crowd watched, Stewart stepped up to the ball, stroked it beautifully, and there was no doubt about the result. When it found the bottom of the cup, he pumped his fist forward while simultaneously kicking his leg backward. The pose, which followed the longest putt to ever win a US Open on the final hole, is one of the most iconic images in the history of the sport and is now immortalized in bronze at the Pinehurst course.

Fate prevented Payne from defending his 1999 US Open title. He died tragically in a plane crash only months after his victory, his loss deeply felt by the golf world. William Payne Stewart will be long remembered for his excellence in golf as well as his jaunty sense of style and mischievous grin. But it was his magical putt on the final hole at the 1999 US Open that has left a breathtaking, indelible moment in the centuries-old history of golf.

US Open Greatness

John Laurence Miller, US Open

John Laurence Miller was born on April 29, 1947, in San Francisco, California. Known to all as "Johnny," he learned to play the game under the tutelage of his father, Larry, a choice that would prove to pay huge dividends. Miller would later say of the father-son coaching relationship, "I was lucky because my father was always positive and never pushed. He always called me 'Champ.'" As Johnny's game progressed, the job of coach was passed to John Geertson, who was instrumental in shaping Miller's idiosyncratic early wrist-cock takeaway. The pairing would prove fruitful as Miller's game flourished, eventually leading to a US Junior Amateur Championship in 1964 and a subsequent collegiate stint at Brigham Young University where he was an All-American.

With Miller's game on the rise, he turned professional in 1969 at the age of twenty-two. Great things were expected of him. The world was his oyster, and just two years later, in 1971, he won his first tournament and was hungry for more. Over the next two years he had only one more tour victory to his credit, but after several strong showings he was knocking at the door of the 1973 US Open at Oakmont.

And it would be at the United States's biggest golf stage where the American Miller would shine brightest. Initially paired with the legendary Arnold Palmer, Miller was two under after the first two rounds with a combined 140 total. On day three, though, it looked like the wheels might be coming off. He struggled to a five-over-par 76, leaving him at a cumulative 216, three over par. So going into round four, things were looking bleak. Miller faced a six-shot deficit and a twelfth-place standing. Yet it is said that great champions often rise to meet their largest challenges, and our hero came out of the box on absolute fire.

Miller birdied the first four holes. With pinpoint drives and laser-like iron play, he hit all eighteen greens in regulation. As his round continued to gain momentum, his meteoric climb up the leader board gained the attention of all in attendance. And at day's end Johnny Miller had used a mere twenty-nine putts to post an eight-under 63, considered one of the greatest rounds in US Open history! And when all of the scorecards were signed, Johnny Miller had secured a one-stroke victory. In doing so he passed many of the top players of the day, including future Hall of Famers Arnold Palmer, Jack Nicklaus, Lee Trevino, and Gary Player.

Miller would use his victory at Oakmont as a springboard to one of the most prodigious two years golf has ever seen. In 1974 and 1975 he won a combined twelve tournaments and was said to have hit the ball closer to the pin than any player who has ever played the game. Miller would later say, "It was sort of golfing nirvana. I'd say my average iron shot for three months in 1975 was within 5 feet of my line, and I had the means for controlling distance. I could feel the shot so well."

And then, in 1976, Miller would go on to secure The British Open at Royal Birkdale with a six-stroke victory over Jack Nicklaus and a nineteen-year-old Seve Ballesteros. Following his major victory at The British Open, however, Miller got a case of the "yips" and never regained his championship form.

In 1988 Johnny Miller was inducted into the Golf Hall of Fame. He is currently involved in several business ventures and also works as an outspoken but popular golf analyst for NBC. Yet despite all of Johnny's milestones, his most treasured golf memory has to be that one glorious day in 1973 when he played one of the most magnificent major rounds in the history of the sport!

The Duel in the Sun

Jack Nicklaus and Tom Watson, British Open

As history has proven, Jack Nicklaus and Tom Watson are two of the greatest golfers to ever play the game. Nicklaus holds the all-time Grand Slam record with eighteen major victories to his credit, while Watson captured an impressive eight major titles to sit sixth on the all-time list.

Both men are now well past their primes and looking back on their many accolades. But back in 1977, as they entered The British Open at Turnberry, the fellow Americans were both at the pinnacle of the golfing world. Jack was already considered by many to be the greatest golfer who ever lived with fourteen major titles at the time, and Tom was the reigning Masters Champion. As the golfing world set their eyes on the United Kingdom, Nicklaus and Watson were clearly two of the favorites . . . and they did not disappoint.

Both men played superbly through the first two rounds, leading to a third-round pairing. As the drama heightened, they went stroke for stroke, ending up with matching 65s to share the lead going into day four. And what a round it would be!

Nicklaus struck first with a birdie on the second. And when Watson bogeyed the same hole, Jack jumped to a two-stroke advantage. Later, on the fourth, Nicklaus struck again with another birdie, giving the Golden Bear a commanding three-stoke lead. But Watson roared back with a birdie on the fifth, and then a little bit of fluky lightning on the eighth. As Watson would later state, "That was a lucky putt. If it wasn't dead center, it would have gone 6 or 7 feet by the hole." Tom bogeyed the ninth, however, ending with a 34, one shot off Nicklaus's lead.

On the back nine the two gladiators would go back and forth with Nicklaus sinking a 22-foot birdie on the twelfth, and Watson coming right back with a 12-foot birdie of his own on thirteen. And when Tom sank a breathtaking 60-foot birdie on fifteen, the two combatants were tied again with three holes to play.

Then came an unforgettable moment. While waiting to tee off on the sixteenth, the two men demonstrated the epitome of camaraderie and competition. Instead of trying to intimidate with a somber demeanor, Watson turned to his playing partner with a smile and said, "This is what it's all about, isn't it?" And Nicklaus nodded, responding in kind, "You bet it is!"

Sixteen ended in a draw, but on the par five seventeenth Watson would get home in two and subsequently two-putt for birdie. And when Jack missed a knee-knocking 3-footer, Tom entered eighteen with a tenuous one-shot advantage.

On the seventy-second hole Watson had the honors and he took full advantage, finding the fairway by smoothing a conservative one iron off the tee. This put Nicklaus on the spot, forcing him to take the aggressive option of launching his tee shot well beyond Watson's, but his driver failed him. He found the deep rough, the ball settling next to a gorse bush. And when Watson struck a pure seven iron, it was all but over as his ball ended up 2 feet from the cup.

Nicklaus wasn't about to lie down, however. With a true champion's spirit, Jack took a mighty swipe and his ball miraculously found the green. That was the good news. The bad news was that it settled 35 feet from the cup. But once more Jack showed his mettle. He took his time, sized up the putt from multiple angles, stood over the ball, adjusted his stance, and executed his typical confident stroke. The crowd began to murmur as the ball tracked its way to the hole, the murmur growing to an excited buzz, a rumble, and finally exploding into a thunderous roar as the ball found the bottom of the cup.

The spectators were still frenzied as Watson lined up his putt for the title. But Nicklaus, in yet another gentlemanly display of courtesy and class, raised his hands to quiet the crowd while Watson went on to sink the winning putt. Nicklaus then put his arm around the victor's shoulder and the two heroes walked to the scorer's tent amidst the crowd's warm applause.

Watson and Nicklaus made golf history that day. The terrific '77 contest at Turnberry would later be referred to as "The Duel in the Sun," and is widely considered one of the finest battles in the history of The British Open.

Sand-tastic

Robert Raymond Tway IV, PGA Championship

Robert Raymond Tway IV was born on May 4, 1959, in Oklahoma City, Oklahoma.

At the age of five Bob was introduced to the game by his father and grandfather, and after a stellar junior career, he entered the Oklahoma State University, where he was part of two National Championships and was a three-time, first team All-American. Shortly after graduation he turned to the pro tour, where big things were expected from the Okie sensation, but like many rookies he failed to find immediate success.

In 1983, at the tour-qualifying tournament on the TPC course in Ponte Vera, Florida, there was a devastating setback. Sitting in twelfth place as he entered the sixth and final round, Tway must have been confident that he would end up in the top fifty, all of whom would gain their tour cards. But it was not to be. On the final day his game came apart, and to add insult to injury he double bogeyed the eighteenth to shoot an 81, failing to qualify by just one painful shot.

Bob Tway had never been a quitter, though. He redoubled his efforts and came back the following year to earn his coveted card. And just two years later, in 1986, he would have the most magical season of his career. On February 9, he won in a playoff over Bernhard Langer at the Shearson Lehman Brothers Andy Williams

Open. And following that milestone, he scored two more tour victories prior to entering the PGA Championship at Toledo's Inverness course in Ohio.

Looking for his first major title, Tway managed to play consistent golf for rounds one and two, coming in with a 72 and 70. Then on day three, lightning struck. Tway came out on fire and played like a man possessed for the entire round. His sizzling score, a record 64, launched him into contention for the title.

The weatherman took a bit away from Tway's momentum, however, as the final was pushed back a day due to a Sunday rainout. And to make his task all the more daunting, Tway was still looking up at Greg Norman, the year's other dominant golfer, who began the round with a four-shot advantage. Well behind going to the back nine, Tway gained four strokes in eight holes on the Australian as Norman began to falter. It left the two leaders tied at seven under par going into the seventy-second and final hole of the tournament.

After a clean shot off the tee, Norman put his second shot 25 feet from the pin on the 354-yard par four. The situation looked a bit bleak for Tway when his approach found the greenside bunker. He kept a calm demeanor, however. After surveying the situation he dug in, took one more look at the pin, and sliced his sand wedge beneath the ball. The result . . . Tway's ball popped out, landed softly onto the lightning-fast green, and the crowd gasped as it tracked directly toward the pin and found the bottom of the cup for a birdie three! As the normally reserved Tway jumped up and down, the crowd roared its approval. And when Norman missed his long birdie attempt, it was all over. Bob Tway had holed out from the bunker on the seventy-second hole to win the PGA Championship in one of the most memorable shots in the history of the sport!

Despite the fact that Norman led all four majors after three rounds in 1986, a feat that would come to be known as "The Saturday

Slam," he would end up victorious at only one of those events, that year's British Open. In the end it would be Tway who would walk away with the Player of the Year honors.

Bob Tway would win only four more PGA Titles throughout his career. Yet it was that one magical moment in 1986 that will forever define his career and leave him with the immortal title of PGA Champion!

Splish, Splash

T.J. Moore, Dryden Invitational

Sometimes, the words "golf" and "frustrating" are synonymous. And your humble author is just a weekend hacker with a double-digit handicap! So just imagine that you're up against the myriad vagaries that a round of golf presents to you, and on top of that you're playing to earn a living! Pity those poor pros! With their livelihoods on the line and the pressure of playing in front of huge galleries, the tension must be nearly unbearable. On top of the world one minute and crashing back to earth the next, and only because your swing was a quarter inch off line. And meanwhile the galleries, as well as the tournament officials, demand gentlemanly behavior even when you've blown a chance at serious money.

As Rudyard Kipling famously stated, "If you can meet with triumph and disaster, and treat those two imposters just the same . . . yours is the earth and everything that's in it, and which is more, you'll be a man, my son." Well, these inspirational words were never more appropriate than in the 1978 Dryden Invitational, which was played at the Port Arthur Country Club in Texas.

As the tournament got under way, the forty-nine-year-old amateur T.J. Moore must have been happy with his round. After all, he was playing "pretty good golf" as he approached the 381-yard par four eighteenth hole.

But when Moore played his third shot from 75 yards out, he found a bit of difficulty when his ball hit one of the large ponds that protect the green. He remained unfazed, however. He calmly reached into his bag, grabbed another ball, took his drop, and fired away again. The result was the same . . . kerplunk! And then it happened again . . . and again . . . and again! Although Moore was ready to throw in the towel, his playing partners continued to encourage him, and he simply wouldn't give up. Amazingly, after going through all twelve balls in his bag, his playing partners loaned him more, and to his credit, Moore kept at it although the result was regrettably the same.

Finally, in an act of sheer mercy, Moore's twenty-first wedge shot found the green as the crowd roared its approval. After two-putting, Moore scurried off the green and into the club house to assess the damage. With his twenty-five strokes, not to mention twenty more due to penalty, T.J. Moore chalked up an incredible 45 for the hole.

Yet despite the ordeal, Moore was somehow able to keep his composure, and for his efforts he was awarded the tournament's good sportsmanship award. I'm sure somewhere Rudyard Kipling was smiling.

Pocket Panic

Cary Middlecoff, Palm Beach Round Robin Tournament

Cary Middlecoff was born on January 26, 1921, in Halls, Tennessee. Despite the fact that he never had a lesson, the young Cary developed an epic command of the game. After graduating from Christian Brothers High School, he moved on to the University of Mississippi, where he became the university's first golf All-American in 1939. He then won the Tennessee State Amateur Championship over four successive years from 1940 to 1943.

Dr. Middlecoff, a licensed dentist, served in World War II, where he filled approximately seven thousand teeth. This painstakingly mundane experience convinced him to give professional golf a try, and it would be a life-altering decision. He would go on to win an incredible forty professional tournaments, including two US Open titles (1949 and 1956) and a Masters title in 1955. The 1950s were an especially prolific time. In a decade that featured such golf luminaries as Ben Hogan and Sam Snead, Dr. Cary Middlecoff (as he was usually referred to) racked up twenty-eight tour victories, which was more than any other player during that time period. He would also play on three Ryder Cup teams (1953, 1955, and 1959).

With all of Middlecoff's accolades, who would have expected that an incredible moment would occur at the inauspicious 1952 Palm Beach Round Robin Tournament at the Wykagyl Country Club in New Rochelle, New York? But if this book has taught us anything, it's that virtually anything can occur in golf, at virtually any place or time, and this astonishing moment is no different.

The gifted Middlecoff was leading the round-robin tournament on the sixteenth hole when he hit a shot that went amiss. Incredibly, the wayward ball landed directly into the pocket of an unsuspecting patron! The spectator, apparently shaken at the turn of events, took the ball out his pocket, threw it into some deep rough, and subsequently ran away. Cary was shocked as he watched the situation unfold, but after consulting with tournament officials, there was nothing he could do but play the ball where it lay. Despite his best efforts at hacking out of the jungle-like rough, he double bogeyed the hole, and as a direct result of the reaction of the panicked spectator, he lost the tournament.

Dr. Cary Middlecoff was a dentist turned golfer who ended his days on the professional links as one of the best players of his generation, and in the culmination of a scintillating career, he was inducted into the Golf Hall of Fame in 1986. He is also remembered for a quirky turn of events in 1952 that cost him a tournament title. But revenge is sweet, and the good doctor would have it the following year when he entered the same Palm Beach Round Robin and walked away with the title!

Caddie Doghouse

Eddie Martin and Byron Nelson, US Open

It has often been said that those who can't do, teach. Well, in the golfing world—if you don't have the talent to earn a playing card on tour—teaching isn't your only option. Finding a niche as a caddie isn't such a bad consolation prize. In today's high-money game, the top caddies can earn nearly seven figures. And if one holds the idea that caddieing is a relatively pressure-free profession, life as a professional caddie would be considered a pretty good gig. Truly, what could go wrong? Well, if that question was posed to Byron Nelson's caddie, Eddie Martin, right after the 1946 US Open, he'd most likely give you an earful regarding the perils involved with carrying the bag.

Byron Nelson was a superstar in his day, and is still considered to have been one of the best to play the game. And even during the mid part of the twentieth century, when the money earned as a caddie was a mere fraction of what it is today, the right to carry the great Byron Nelson's clubs was still a coveted prize.

At the 1946 US Open, Nelson's short career was coming to an end, and he surely wanted to go out with one more major title. Things were looking good for Lord Byron as he was in contention throughout the event. But during the third round, as he laid up at the par five thirteenth hole at Canterbury, caddie Eddie Martin lost his balance as he ducked under a rope used to hold back the gallery and inadvertently kicked Nelson's ball. The instant result was a one-shot penalty stroke, but the true repercussions wouldn't be felt until the end of the tournament.

As you may have guessed, this innocent mistake ended up being very costly. Nelson seemed destined to win the tournament outright, but with the penalty stroke added onto his scorecard, he ended up tied for the lead with Vic Ghezzi and Lloyd Mangrum. Then, in an even more painful turn of events, Nelson would lose the thirty-six-hole playoff by a single stroke to Mangrum.

After the event, a distraught Nelson turned to the radio announcer, Bill Stern, whose broadcast was sponsored by Gillette razors. "Bill," he said, "just give me one of those things you're advertising and I'll cut my throat."

Eddie Martin may have originally felt as if he was one lucky man when he was picked to carry the great Byron Nelson's bag. But after the tournament concluded, one can only assume that Martin would have preferred to crawl right inside the bag himself.

What a Pest

Lloyd Eugene Mangrum, US Open

Lloyd Eugene Mangrum was born on August 1, 1914, in Trenton, Texas. With his smooth swing and calm, cool demeanor, Mangrum was aptly known as "The Icicle." He joined the PGA Tour in 1937, and despite the fact that his career was interrupted by World War II, Lloyd was still able to secure an amazing thirty-six tour titles throughout his illustrious career.

Although Mangrum's war experience was harrowing (he won four battle stars, two Purple Hearts, and was wounded in the Battle of the Bulge), his best golfing years came after those years in combat. As mentioned in the previous story ("Caddie Doghouse"), Mangrum won his only major at the 1946 US Open with a little bit of luck when Byron Nelson's caddie, Eddie Martin, inadvertently kicked Nelson's ball. Yet I believe the expression "What goes around comes around" would aptly portray what happened next.

In the 1950 US Open, Mangrum was in contention for his second major title. Throughout the four rounds he played inspired golf, and at the end he found himself in a three-way playoff with Ben Hogan and George Fazio. As the playoff round was coming to a close, Mangrum was only one stroke off the lead coming into the par four sixteenth hole. While lining up his putt for par, he was momentarily distracted as a gnat landed on his ball, so he picked up his ball, blew off the little pest, and went on to drain the 15-footer. When Hogan sank his par as well, Mangrum assumed that he was still just one shot off the lead with two holes to play.

But not so fast! The US Golf Association Rule's Committee Chair, Isaac Grainger, informed Mangrum that the rule at the time stated that a golfer cannot lift a ball that is in play, and if he does so he shall be assessed a two-stroke penalty. Mangrum was completely unaware of the rule, and in a cruel twist of events, Hogan cruised to victory.

Although Mangrum was forced into an early retirement due to a series of heart attacks, his overall body of work holds up quite nicely against almost anyone's. Along with his US Open victory in 1946, he led the tour money list in 1951 and captured the Vardon Trophy that same year for achieving the lowest scoring average. Lloyd was also a US representative on six Ryder Cup teams and served as its captain in 1951. And in 1998, Lloyd Mangrum was posthumously inducted into Golf's Hall of Fame. He was a giant of the game, but it was a pesky little gnat that might have cost him a win at the 1950 US Open!

Chip Shot

Larry Mize, The Masters

If you happen to be born in the shadow of one of golf's most famous venues, it is only natural to dream of competing there one day, and maybe even walking away with the title. Such was the case with Lawrence Hogan "Larry" Mize, who was born on September 23, 1958, in Augusta, Georgia, home of the venerated Masters Tournament. As a youngster Larry took up the game of golf, often fantasizing about playing at his home town tournament. And his game developed nicely, leading to an impressive collegiate career at Georgia Tech, after which he turned pro in 1980.

Mize was far from a sensation on the PGA tour, however. In fact he was a perennial grinder, somehow managing to keep his tour card by repeatedly finishing each year among the top twenty-five money winners. Given his performance history, Larry entered the 1987 Masters with scant hope of taking the title he had so often dreamed of.

To everyone's surprise Mize was in the hunt all the way, and after scoring a birdie on the tournament's seventy-second hole, the last hole on the last day, he found himself in a playoff with two of the giants of the game, namely Greg Norman and Seve Ballesteros. So even in the sudden death format, Larry Mize was an afterthought. How could he even have the temerity to stand on the same hallowed ground next to the other top finishers? After all, Norman was the number one player in the world, Ballesteros was ranked third, and Mize was a distant thirty-sixth. Even more daunting, Norman and Ballesteros came into the playoff with a total of ninety-one combined worldwide tournament victories. Meanwhile, the unheralded Mize had only one win, which he had secured at the Danny Thomas Memphis Classic.

Nevertheless, Mize continued to hang around, and when Seve bogeyed the tenth, it was down to just Larry and Greg Norman, *mano a mano,* for what many view as the world's most prestigious golf title. And then came the seemingly inevitable. On number seventeen it appeared that Larry's dream would surely come up short, his ball missing the green and landing well right, while Norman's shot found the front edge.

As Mize took stock of the situation, he knew things looked ominous. He kept his composure, however, and after careful consideration decided to play a bump and run with a 56-degree wedge. As he later stated, "I picked a spot and landed it right there." The little white sphere tracked laser-like toward the pin while the crowd held its collective breath, then exploded into an ear-splitting roar as the ball found the bottom of the cup for a birdie. The scene was nearly riotous. Mize immediately soared from the ground in a jubilant leap, then romped around the green in fist-pumping ecstasy, an unforgettable moment that was fortunately recorded on videotape and has been replayed thousands upon thousands of times.

It took seemingly forever for the frenzied crowd to calm down and allow Norman a chance to tie with a birdie of his own. But fate had already decided the outcome. Norman's putt missed and the journeyman Larry Mize, the kid who grew up just minutes from the verdant fairways of Augusta Country Club, had been chosen by the golfing gods to wear the coveted green jacket.

Mize would go on to win two more tournaments in his PGA career for a total of just four victories, and as of this writing he plays on the Champions Tour. But for his singular moment of fame, he might have quietly faded from golf history. That one incredible chip shot has immortalized the name of Larry Mize, and is now remembered as one of the most miraculous moments in the history of the Masters.

Master Meltdown

James B. Ferrier, The Masters

The Land Down Under has contributed a number of luminaries to the world of golf. Among them was a talented fellow by the name of James B. Ferrier, who was born on February 24, 1915, in the city of Sydney, Australia. Jim's father, an accomplished golfer in his own right, introduced his son to the game. And in an example of "like father, like son," the younger Ferrier quickly picked up the finer points of the game. In his teens a soccer injury left him with a lifelong limp, but despite this handicap he went on to parlay his golfing talent into a professional career.

After moving to the United States in 1940, Ferrier became a regular on the PGA Tour. Four years later he found his first real taste of success when he scored a victory at the Oakland Open in 1944, and three years after that he must have felt as if he was living the American dream when he won his first major tournament, the 1947 PGA Championship.

With additional tour wins in 1947 and 1948, and three more in 1949, Jim entered the 1950 Masters on a crest of confidence. His performance was stellar from the very first tee, and as the celebrated tournament played out, it appeared to all as if the green jacket were in his grasp. At the start of the final round, Ferrier held a four-stroke lead over two-time Masters Champion Jimmy Demaret. And by the time the players got ready to take on the final nine holes, Ferrier had expanded his lead to a commanding five-shot advantage.

It was a foregone conclusion; the title was Ferrier's. But then . . .

The first omen came when Ferrier bogeyed the thirteenth . . . and then the fourteenth . . . and then it got worse. Much worse. He double-bogeyed the sixteenth and continued his downward spiral by also bogeying the seventeenth and eighteenth. When all was said and done, Ferrier had ended the back nine with a horrific 41, and in the process had lost the title to Demaret in a stunning Masters meltdown!

For his part, Jimmy Demaret became the first three-time Masters winner in the history of the tournament, but the storyline of the day was all about the hapless Ferrier and his epic collapse.

Jim Ferrier would end his career with thirty professional victories, but would never manage to win The Masters, nor any other major other than that 1947 PGA. He passed away on June 13, 1986, at the age of seventy-one, and to date has still not been inducted into the Golf Hall of Fame despite having better credentials than others who have been enshrined. One can't help but think that had Ferrier been able to secure his grasp on the 1950s Masters, he would have been in the Hall of Fame years ago. Oh, what a heart-wrenching game this beautiful sport can be!

Drive for Show, Putt for Dough

Arthur D'Arcy "Bobby" Locke, Putting Streak

As any golfer worth his salt will tell you, it's all well and good to hit big off the tee, but if you don't have an outstanding short game, you'll never become a low handicapper, let alone make it on the tour. This sentiment was personified by the great South African golfer, Arthur D'Arcy "Bobby" Locke. Born on November 20, 1917, in Germiston, South Africa, Bobby had a career that was paralleled by few others. And as you may have guessed by now, Locke made his bread and butter on the putting greens.

Using a very unorthodox putting style, where he would take the putter back far inside and actually make contact with a closed club-face, legend has it that Bobby could literally put spin on his putts to make them hook or slice at will. And his tremendous putting talent took him a long way, leading to nine wins as an amateur and seventy-two victories as a pro. Most notably, he claimed the Claret Jug as the British Open Champion on four separate occasions (1949, 1950, 1952, and 1957).

But of all Bobby Locke's amazing accomplishments, 1945 was truly one of the most incredible stretches in the history of putting statistics. He played a lot of golf that year, and not surprisingly his putter did not disappoint. Now for those of you whose nemesis is three-putting, you might want to sit down before reading the next paragraph.

In what was arguably the most amazing feat in golfing history, Bobby Locke played 1,800 holes that year *without a single three-putt*! And that was not a misprint: *1,800 holes*! Do the math ... *100 rounds of golf*! Seemingly impossible, but the records confirm it.

In 1977, due in large part to his incredible prowess on the greens, Locke became only the second player (after Gary Player) who didn't come from the United Kingdom or the United States to be enshrined into golf's Hall of Fame.

I guess it shouldn't come as a surprise to discover who it was that coined one of the most famous phrases in the world of sport. Yes, it was Bobby Locke who first stated the oft-repeated golf maxim, "You drive for show, but putt for dough."

Grand Slam

Bobby Jones, US Open, British Open, US Amateur,
and British Amateur Championships

Virtually every sports fan knows the name Robert Tyre "Bobby" Jones is synonymous with golf excellence. Born at the turn of the twentieth century on March 17, 1902, in Atlanta, Georgia, Bobby was a sickly child and played golf to help build up his stamina. It was an inauspicious beginning, but what started as an exercise to benefit his health soon evolved into an epic story of heroics and greatness.

The young Bobby Jones was a golf prodigy who won his first tournament at the tender age of six. At fourteen he made the third round of The US Amateur Championship, but the real news was that he was just getting started! Bobby qualified for his first US Open at the age of eighteen, and three years later, in 1923, he would win the event for his first major title. And then, in 1926, he became the first man to win both The British and US Opens in the same year.

Fast-forward to 1930. The United States was mired in the stock market crash and subsequent Great Depression. The population was desperately seeking a positive distraction, and Bobby Jones was just the man to lift their spirits. After winning the British Amateur and British Open, Jones was already a conquering hero, but the golfing world clamored for more and Bobby was up to the task. He entered the US Open and took the third leg of the Grand Slam by defeating Macdonald Smith by two strokes at the Interlachen Country Club in Minnesota.

By the time Jones entered the fourth and final leg of what was poised to be a historic potential major victory, the golfing world was in an absolute frenzy. The pressure was suffocating, but Jones did not disappoint. As 18,000 fans followed his every move at the Merion Crick Club in Haverford, Pennsylvania, Jones annihilated the field and cruised to an 8 and 7 victory over Eugene Homans to capture the US Amateur. In doing so he became the first—and to date the only—man to ever capture golf's Grand Slam.

Since his historic victory in 1930, several of the game's greats have vied to reenact Jones's magical year. Ben Hogan came close in 1953 when he won the first three majors of the year but skipped the fourth leg at the PGA Championships as it conflicted with The British Open. Arnold Palmer won the first half of the Grand Slam in 1960, and Jack Nicklaus did the same in 1972, but both men eventually faltered. And then, in 2000 and 2001 Tiger Woods won four consecutive slam events but failed to do so in the same calendar year. Bobby Jones's amazing feat has held the test of time, and as the years pass its magnitude continues to increase exponentially.

At the end of 1930 Jones had won thirteen major championships in twenty attempts. But then, at the youthful age of twenty-eight and at the peak of his prodigious talent, he stunned the golfing world by announcing that he was retiring from the game.

Jones went on to lead a relatively quiet life, coming out of retirement to play only The Masters. He died on December 18, 1971, and was posthumously inducted into the Golf Hall of Fame in 1974. His Grand Slam triumph in 1930 continues to stand as the hallmark achievement in the history of the sport, and it should come as no surprise that the mere mention of his name evokes an image of golfing prowess. But more than that, Bobby Jones is remembered as a grand gentleman who embodied both dignity and class on and off the golf course, and he will always be thought of not only as a transcendent talent but also as the ultimate ambassador of the game.

The Streak

Byron Nelson,

Consecutive Tournament Championships

When it comes to streaks in the world of sports, a number of extraordinary records come to mind. In baseball, Joe DiMaggio's hitting safely in fifty-six consecutive games. In tennis, Roger Federer's reaching twenty-three Grand Slam semifinals in a row. In boxing, Rocky Marciano's undefeated career as a professional, forty-nine wins without a single loss. But in this author's estimation the streak that is most likely to never be tied or broken is held by the great Byron Nelson.

John Byron Nelson was born on February 4, 1912, in Waxahachie, Texas. His childhood saw a brush with death when he contracted typhoid fever as an eleven-year-old and lost nearly half his body weight to the disease. Thankfully he recovered, and soon after his baptism at age twelve he began to caddie at the Glen Garden Country Club. Club rules stipulated that caddies weren't permitted to play on their course, and so the resourceful young Byron played at night. Legend has it that he would put his white handkerchief over the hole so he could see it in the darkness. A couple years later, the club changed its policy, Nelson was free to develop his craft, and he eventually turned professional in 1932. Five years later, in 1937, "Lord Byron," as he would come to be known, secured his first major victory at The Masters.

Flash forward to 1945 when Nelson was at his peak. The beginning of the year saw him finish either first or second in his first eight tournaments. In Jacksonville, however, he finished sixth, and apparently this mild setback didn't sit well. Just about a week later, on March 14, he won the Miami International Four-Ball Tournament, and although those in attendance were unaware of it at the time, they had just witnessed the beginning of arguably the greatest streak in the history of sports.

Now the floodgates opened. At his next tournament, Nelson would win the Charlotte Open, and then, consecutively, The Greater Greensboro Open; The Durham Open; The Atlanta Open; The Montreal Open; The Philadelphia Inquirer; The Chicago Victory National Open; The PGA Championship (which was the only major played that year due to World War II); The Tam O'Shanter Open; and the Canadian Open.

Count 'em: *eleven tournaments in a row*! On August 19, 1945, the streak would come to an end when Nelson finished fourth at Memphis, but the magnitude of this nearly half year of pure golfing brilliance speaks for itself. In the nearly seventy years since Nelson's accomplishment, no other golfer has even come within a sniff of this astounding record.

Nelson's performance in 1945 is universally acknowledged as the greatest year ever played on the PGA Tour. Not only did he win eleven straight tournaments, but he also had *a total* of eighteen victories with seven second-place finishes for the year. Perhaps even more amazing, he shot nineteen consecutive rounds under 70 with a scoring average of 68.33 (67.45 in the fourth round). Ask any golfer; this is truly mind-boggling. The great Arnold Palmer was quoted as saying, "I don't think that anyone will ever exceed the things that Byron did by winning eleven tournaments in a row in one year." And more recently Tiger Woods called the Nelson feat, "One of the greatest years in the history of the sport."

Byron was inducted in to the Golf Hall of Fame in 1974 and died on September 26, 2006. Less than a month after his death, President George W. Bush posthumously presented Nelson with the Congressional Gold Medal.

Byron Nelson is remembered for many things. He was a deeply religious man who was a true gentleman on and off the golf course. And of course he was one of the best golfers to ever play the game. But Lord Byron will always be remembered, first and foremost, for his amazing streak of eleven straight tournament victories. According to the old saw, "Records are made to be broken," but the odds are astronomical that this one won't stand the test of time.

The Record

Jack Nicklaus, Major Championships

Records may be meant to be broken, but in golf there's one record that holds a sacred status. The number is 18, and it's held by none other than The Golden Bear, aka Jack Nicklaus.

Jack William Nicklaus was born on January 21, 1940 in Columbus, Ohio. A gifted all-around athlete, young Jack took up the game of golf at age ten. On the first nine holes he ever played, he shot an amazing 51 and never looked back, winning the first of five consecutive Ohio state junior titles at the age of twelve. At thirteen he was the year's youngest qualifier at the US Junior Amateur; at fourteen he won the Tri-State High School Championship (Ohio, Kentucky, and Indiana); at fifteen he shot a course record 66 at his country club; and at sixteen, in 1956, he won the Ohio Open. All in all, from the ages of ten to seventeen Jack Nicklaus won twenty-seven events in the greater Ohio area.

Nicklaus would go on to attend Ohio State University and would win the US Amateur in 1959, and both the NCAA and US Amateur titles in 1961. After deciding to turn professional late in 1961, Jack left Ohio State University just a few courses short of graduating. It seemed like a rash decision at the time, but in retrospect it turned out to be arguably the best decision of Jack's young life. To support this statement, in just the seventeenth tournament he entered as a pro, the 1962 US Open at Oakmont, he won his first major title in a Sunday playoff over the legendary Arnold Palmer. And he was just getting started . . .

Jack would go on to win The Masters and PGA Championship in 1963, and The Masters again in 1965 and 1966. When he won The British Open in 1966, the twenty-six-year-old Nicklaus became the youngest player to ever achieve the career Grand Slam. A year later, in 1967, he would again win the US Open, and after a minor dry spell he would next win yet another major at The British Open in 1970.

As history would prove, the 1970s would be Nicklaus's most prolific decade as a major championship winner. In 1971 he would win the PGA Championship, then both The Masters and US Open in 1972. In 1973 Jack would win the PGA Championship and in doing so would break the great Bobby Jones's major championship record. He would follow that up with his fifth Masters victory in 1975, and win the PGA Championship again that year as well. After winning The British Open again in 1978 and The US Open and PGA title in 1980, it appeared as if The Golden Bear's prolific run of majors would come to an end. But Jack had one more treat in store for us. Six years later, at the age of forty-six, Nicklaus would thrill the golfing world by capturing his sixth Masters victory and eighteenth overall major title . . . an all-time record that still stands!

Jack Nicklaus was inducted into the Golf Hall of Fame in 1974. Golfers and sports historians generally agree that Nicklaus is the greatest to ever play the game. There have been other contenders, most notably the colossally talented Tiger Woods, but Jack's supporters simply smile confidently and point to that nearly unassailable record: eighteen major titles!

I have a five-dollar bill that says it's never going to be surpassed, even by Tiger.

Any takers?

From Tragedy to Triumph

Ben Hogan, Heroics on and off the Course

Some moments are a lifetime in the making. Such was the case with a man who was the dominant figure of golf in the middle of the twentieth century. In the late '40s and the early '50s, the name Ben Hogan was practically synonymous with golf, and he is still considered by golf historians and casual fans alike to be one of the greatest players in the history of the sport. However, when one considers his path to greatness, Hogan's future legendary status would have been hard to predict.

William Ben Hogan was born on August 13, 1912, in Dublin, Texas, and was the last of three children born to Chester and Clara Hogan. Tragically, when Ben was only nine his father committed suicide, resulting in emotional and financial disaster for the Hogan family. The traumatized children would have to pitch in while their seamstress mother struggled to keep them afloat. Initially Ben contributed by delivering newspapers, but at age eleven he got a job as a caddie, a seemingly minor development that would eventually have a revolutionary impact on the sport of golf.

With the steely dedication and the opportunity to hone his skills on a legitimate golf course, Ben was a quick study, mastering the intricacies of the game. Eventually he dropped out of Central High School during the final semester of his senior year and turned professional more than six months before his eighteenth birthday.

There would be tough times ahead. It would be nearly a decade before he won his first professional tournament at the Hershey Four Ball in 1938. But then, bolstered by his success, in 1940 Hogan would win three consecutive tournaments, and his career began to take off. In 1946 Hogan would win his first major title at the PGA Championship. This was followed in 1948 by another PGA victory in addition to a US Open title. And then, with the golfing world seemingly in the palm of his hand, tragedy struck again.

On February 2, 1949, while driving on a fog-drenched bridge, Hogan and his wife, Valerie, crashed into a bus in a head-on collision. Ben was said to have thrown himself across his wife in an attempt to protect her. In doing so, incredibly, he saved not only her life but also his own. The steering column punctured the driver's seat. Still, the thirty-six-year-old Hogan sustained devastating injuries. As a result of the accident Hogan was left with a double fracture of the pelvis, a fractured collar bone, a rib injury, a fracture of the left ankle, and a nearly fatal complication of life-threatening blood clots. Initially his doctors stated that he might never walk again, let alone play professional golf. But Ben Hogan's legendary determination would prevail as he left the hospital only fifty-nine days later, and as history would later prove, his best days were still ahead of him.

It took only one year to return to his previous status. Ben won The US Open in 1950, and in 1951 he repeated in The Open and won The Masters as well. Then, in 1953, Hogan dominated the sport like few have done before or since. That magical year saw him win three more major titles, and he was denied a chance at the Grand Slam only because the fourth major, the PGA Championship, conflicted with The British Open.

Over the course of his stellar career, Ben Hogan would win sixty-four PGA tournaments and nine major titles. Still considered by many as the ultimate luminary in the history of the sport, he would be inducted into the Golf Hall of Fame in 1974. But as impressive as his golf legend came to be, it is almost dwarfed by the bravery and determination he showed in dealing with the terrible personal obstacles he was forced to overcome. Small wonder that he is remembered for his stunning courage as well as his excellence in golf.

Ben Hogan: a legend in golf, and a hero in life.

The Merry Mex

Lee Trevino, US Open, Canadian Open,

and British Open

It is said that some men were born to be great, and some had greatness thrust upon them.

One might also say that in certain cases, a man becomes great when no one saw it coming. The latter statement holds true for Lee Buck Trevino.

Lee Trevino's origins were humble. He was born on December 1, 1939, in Dallas, Texas, into a family of Mexican ancestry. His father left the family during Lee's formative years, resulting in Lee being raised by his mother, Juanita, and his grandfather, Joe Trevino, who made his living as a grave digger.

As legend has it, Lee was introduced to the game when he found an abandoned five iron with a wooden shaft and began to hit "horse apples" (aka dehydrated horse manure). He was in the habit of attending school sporadically, spending his days honing his golf talent at the Hardy Greenwood driving range and par three golf course. He then served two terms with the Marines, after which he landed a job as a club professional in El Paso, Texas. His game flourished, leading to a decision to try his luck on the professional tour, and just one year later Lee would win the prestigious US Open at the Oak Hill Country Club in Rochester, New York. Although this victory must have seemed like a dream come true for a young man from such a modest background, Lee took it in stride. In fact, he was just getting started.

With his winning personality this charismatic player was dubbed "The Merry Mex," and soon he was featured in advertisements all over the world. Yet Trevino never let his success get to his head. He was said to have a prodigious work ethic, and his dedication was about to pay off in a big way.

In 1971 Trevino entered The US Open at the Merion Golf Club in Philadelphia, Pennsylvania. His performance was nothing short of inspired, and after four rounds of 70, 72, 69, and 69, he found himself in a tie with the great Jack Nicklaus. To most golfers, the prospect of coming face-to-face with The Golden Bear would have been intimidating, but Lee was not cowed. He won handily by three shots in the eighteen-hole playoff.

Two weeks later Trevino would enter The Canadian Open at the Richelieu Valley Golf Course and Country Club in the province of Quebec. After four more solid rounds of 73, 68, 67, and 67, he once again found himself in a playoff, this time with Art Wall Jr. The result was the same, with Trevino winning again in a playoff for his second national championship in as many tournaments. But as you may have guessed, The Merry Mex wasn't done. Not by a long shot!

Just a few days later he crossed the Atlantic to test his luck at The British Open. The tournament that year was held at the formidable Royal Birkdale Golf Club, where he shot four brilliant rounds of 69, 70, 69, and 70 to defeat Lul Liang-Huan by a single stroke. In case there had been any doubt about his staying power, Lee Trevino became the first man to win these three national championships in the same year, and he did it in a one-month span!

Lee would go on to win six major championships and was enshrined into the Golf Hall of Fame in 1981. But it was ten years earlier that The Merry Mex accomplished a stunning string of victories over three glorious weeks, and by doing so he left his personal, indelible mark on golf history.

Take Two Aspirin

Harry Vardon, British Open

Lest we forget that the game of golf has been around for some time, let's travel back in time to May 9, 1870, the birthdate of Harry Vardon in Grouville, Jersey, Channel Islands. Despite the meager circumstances of the Vardon family, and over the strenuous objections of their father, both Harry and his brother Tom indicated early on that they were interested in pursuing the game of golf as a career. This was hardly the sort of ambition fostered by folks who were struggling to put food on their table, but against all odds both brothers were successful at pursuing the game they loved. After learning the finer points of golf as a caddie, Harry followed his brother to England in 1890 to take a job as a greenskeeper for a club in Yorkshire. And it wouldn't be long before Harry was a superstar.

In 1896, Harry came back from a fifty-four-hole, four-shot deficit to take his first Open Championship in a playoff over J.H. Taylor. And while the feat was impressive in its own right, it turned out to be just the beginning. Two years later Vardon would come from behind again, this time after trailing by two shots after the third round to claim his second British Open by one stroke over Willie Park Jr. And a year later he was victorious once more as he claimed his third Open Championship with a five-stroke margin of victory. The poor boy from the Channel Islands had claimed victory in three British Opens before his thirtieth birthday! But the best was yet to come, albeit with a "major" incident along the way.

After winning The US Open in 1900, Harry went through a slump that lasted for three years, so one can surely bet that he was itching for another title as he entered the 1903 Open Championships. The good news was that Harry was at the top of his game as he built a commanding seven-shot lead through the first fifty-four holes. The bad news? Vardon was so weakened by tuberculosis that he was literally stumbling through his final round, nearly fainting on several occasions. Amazingly, he was able to muster his way to his fourth Open Championship title, winning by six strokes over his brother Tom but was actually admitted to a TB sanitarium after the tournament!

Thankfully, Vardon made a full recovery and eight years later would come back full circle to win his fifth Open Championship, this time in a playoff over Arnaud Massy. And in case this wasn't impressive enough, he would win his record sixth, and final, Open in 1914 with a three-stroke margin of victory over J.H. Taylor.

Although much of his career preceded the establishment of the PGA in 1916, Harry Vardon won an impressive sixty-two tournaments, including a stretch of fourteen in a row. He would pass away on March 20, 1937, at the age of sixty-six, and in 1974 would be posthumously enshrined into the Golf Hall of Fame. But perhaps his most extraordinary accomplishment was the example of stunning courage when he fought both a challenging golf course and the devastating disease of tuberculosis to capture one of the most coveted titles in all of sports.

British Brilliance

Tom Watson, British Open

Thomas Sturges Watson comes from the "Show Me" state of Missouri. He was born on September 4, 1949, in Kansas City, and as a youngster, Tom's father, Ray, introduced him to the game that would make him famous. As you might expect, Tom was a natural and found immediate success. As his game continued to flourish, the accolades followed, most notably in his early career with four straight Missouri State Amateur Championships from 1968 through 1971. After starring at Stanford University and graduating with a degree in psychology, Watson would eventually turn professional and join the PGA Tour in 1971.

Tom encountered disappointment early in his pro career, but he managed to establish himself by taking the lead into the last round of the 1974 US Open at Winged Foot. At this point, however, it appeared as if nerves got the best of him and he finished the tournament well out of contention. Although this sort of experience can be devastating, Tom didn't hang his head. Just two weeks later, at The Western Open, he came roaring back from a final round six-shot deficit to claim his first tour title. He had finally made his mark, and the best was yet to come.

The following year, in 1975, Watson would etch his name into golfing immortality by taking his first major title at The British Open at Carnoustie. And two years later, in 1977, he secured his second

Open Championship, defeating Jack Nicklaus at Turnberry in Scotland in an event many golf historians consider to be the greatest tournament played in the second half of the twentieth century. At the age of twenty-five, well before the time when many golfers peak, Watson had already locked up two major victories at the game's oldest major. But he wasn't finished, not by a long shot!

In 1980 he claimed yet another title, this time at the Muirfield Course, and two years later Watson extended his UK streak by winning Open number four at Royal Troon. So how long could this go on, and what were the odds of claiming even another victory? It didn't take long for that question to be answered, for the following year he defended his title with a victory at the Royal Birkdale Golf Club. This was his fifth, and what would ultimately be his final, British Open Championship. There was one other modern day player who also claimed five Open wins, namely Peter Thompson, who did so in the 1960s, but Watson won his titles on five different courses! And he came close to making history yet again when, at the age of fifty-nine, he was literally one putt away from claiming his sixth title at the 2009 Open, but alas it was not to be as Watson faltered, eventually losing in a playoff to Stewart Cink.

Despite that disappointment in 2009, Watson's greatness cannot be denied. He has won seventy professional titles to date, thirty-nine on the PGA tour, with a total of eight majors among them. He has been named the PGA player of the year on six different occasions and was inducted into the Golf Hall of Fame in 1988. At one point, when he appeared unbeatable and was chalking up victory upon victory, the media dubbed him "Tom Terrific." But when one mentions the name of Tom Watson, his brilliance at The British Open always comes to mind. Oh, and did I forget to mention that Watson is currently the holder of three Senior British Open victories as well? Truly incredible!

Tom Terrific

Tom Watson, US Open

The US Open of 1982 happened to be the eighty-second time this tournament was held. It also happened to be only the second Open (and third major) to be played at the historic Pebble Beach Golf Links.

Tom Watson was one of the favorites that year, having entered with an impressive resume that included five career major victories. Watson was also the current number one golfer in the world, but despite this impressive record he had yet to secure his country's national championship. Not that he hadn't come close. In his previous eight appearances he had six top-ten finishes. But as they say, "close" counts only in horseshoes and hand grenades, so he was still chasing that elusive first title.

In his first round Watson was three over through fourteen holes, and it looked as though he might be in for yet another US Open disappointment. But as any golfer can tell you, a round can turn on a dime, and Watson caught fire with three birdies on the final four holes, ending the day with a respectable 72, just two back of the first-round leaders.

In round two Tom struggled again, but his trusty putter repeatedly bailed him out, twice saving bogey from over 20 feet. Afterward he would say, "I shot a 77 and scored a 72." Although he had yet to find his "A game," he still found himself in contention at the beginning of the weekend.

A minor swing adjustment magically changed his performance, and the proof was on the scorecard. His third round posting of 68 was the best among the leaders, leaving him tied for first as he entered the final day of competition.

But lurking close behind, only three shots back, was the dangerous Jack Nicklaus. And when The Golden Bear made a charge with birdies on three, four, five, six, and seven, he was right in the thick of things with Watson and Bill Rogers, who was also vying for the coveted title. Eventually, however, Rogers would falter and the tournament would come down to two of the all-time greats . . . Nicklaus and Watson.

The unflappable Nicklaus performed beautifully, shooting a masterful round of 69. One certainly couldn't have blamed him for feeling pleased with himself as he sat in the clubhouse with a final tally of four under par, more than enough to win most US Opens. Meanwhile, Watson was also at four under when he approached number seventeen, a notoriously difficult par three. The hole lived up to its nasty reputation as Tom's two-iron tee shot went awry and found the deep rough above the green. Now he faced a formidable challenge. The slightest error in his chip could leave the ball in the rough, or happily rolling downhill past the cup.

Either could lead to a double bogey, so Watson's caddie, Bruce Edwards, acutely aware of the danger, cautioned Tom to simply "Get it close," hoping that his man could somehow manage to make par.

But champions are made of different stuff than the rest of us. While everyone else saw the shot as a potential disaster, Watson famously turned to Edwards with a twinkle in his eye and replied, "Hell, I'm going to sink it." And apparently he wasn't kidding, because he then stroked what many consider to be the most outstanding shot of his career. The crowd erupted as his chip plunked straight into the bottom of the cup, while Watson romped toward the hole wearing his trademark wide grin, putter held aloft in glorious triumph.

As if planning to eliminate any doubt, Tom would go on to also birdie the formidable par five eighteenth, and in doing so capture his only US Open by two strokes. But to this day, Tom Watson's chip-in on number seventeen is widely considered to be one of the most memorable and miraculous moments in US Open history.

The Haig

Walter Charles Hagen, PGA Championship

Walter Charles Hagen was the only boy of five children born to William and Louise Hagen of Rochester, New York. His birthdate was December 21, 1892, and although his parents celebrated having a son, their enthusiasm was tempered by their marginal financial circumstances. Walter's father worked as a millwright and blacksmith in the railroad car shops of Rochester, honest, backbreaking work but productive of only meager pay so that the family struggled to survive. As Walter grew, he became aware of their privation, so in an effort to help he took a job as a caddie at The Country Club of Rochester. While doing so he managed to earn a bit of money, but soon he also longed to improve his own proficiency at the game of golf. This ambition posed a problem, however. At the turn of the twentieth century, if a caddie wished to develop his own game, he had to do so at off-peak hours. Consequently, a young Hagen had to scratch and fight for time on the course. Yet with steely determination and a natural talent, Walter's game flourished to the point where he was eventually hired by his club to give lessons and work in the pro shop. This offered him the chance he was looking for. It wouldn't be long until Hagen was ready for the big time.

At just nineteen years of age Walter made his true professional debut at the 1912 Canadian Open and fared quite well, finishing a respectable eleventh. Impressive success for a first tournament, and although Hagan continued to focus on his golf game, the excellent all-around athlete had a difficult decision to make in 1914. That year the Philadelphia Phillies baseball club offered Hagen a tryout. He was tempted, but after considerable thought he made the gut-wrenching decision to forgo the baseball offer in order to concentrate on golf. This decision would prove to be one of the best of Hagen's life as only a week later he secured his first major title by winning The US Open!

After winning his second US Open in 1919, "The Haig" would win his first PGA Championship title in 1921. The event at that time was in match play format, and Hagen took the title with a 3 and 2 finals victory over his opponent Jim Barnes. (Incidentally, the PGA Championships continued to be a match play event until 1958.) In 1922 and 1923 the great Gene Sarazen would take home the coveted PGA Championship titles, but the following year things were about to change. Walter Hagen would make history by winning the 1924 PGA Championship with another final-round victory, again over Jim Barnes, this time with a two-up victory.

With two PGA titles to his credit, the very next year, in 1925, Hagen defeated William Mehlhorn in the final with a dominating 6 and 5 victory. Now with three titles, and two in a row, Walter was on a roll. His momentum continued through 1926 when he was victorious once again, this time by a final match score of 5 and 3 over Leo Diegel. By this time Hagen's name had become synonymous with excellence in golf. He was at the top of his game and had the hardware to prove it.

As Hagen entered the 1927 PGA Championships, he held the aforementioned four PGA Championship titles as well as claiming the title in two US Opens. But there was even more to come, as he narrowly defeated Joe Turnesa by a final score of one up to win his record *fifth* PGA Championship (which he shares with Jack Nicklaus) and his fourth in a row . . . a record he holds by himself to this day.

Walter Hagen would go on to win the Open Championship again in 1928 and 1929, eventually ending his career with a total of eleven major titles. Largely considered to be one of the greatest golfers ever, it was no surprise that Hagen was enshrined into the Golf Hall of Fame in 1974. His accomplishments in golf were legion, but it was his PGA Championship records that have held the test of time and have secured a well-deserved place for "The Haig" among golf's royalty.

The Hustler

Walter Charles Hagen,

Bravado of a Champion

The early part of the twentieth century saw a rather sharp division between amateur and professional golfers. The amateurs were of the privileged class, gentlemen of means and members of exclusive clubs. The pros, on the other hand, were typically ex-caddies from working-class backgrounds, barely tolerated by golf's elite, who viewed them as second-class citizens, drinkers, and philanderers. In tournaments the pros often weren't permitted to use the facilities in the host club, and sometimes not even allowed to enter through the front door.

Then came along Walter Hagen, who envisioned a more respectable image for the professional game. He encountered considerable resistance, but by virtue of his winning personality as well as his golfing prowess, he began to make some inroads, however slight. In fact, it wasn't until 1920 that the Inverness Club in Toledo, Ohio, responded to Hagen's influence by allowing the participating professionals to use their facilities during a tournament. In response, Hagen organized the pros to pitch in and present the club with a gift of a large grandfather clock.

He was quoted as saying, "My game was my business, and as a business it demanded constant playing in the championship bracket, for a current title was my selling commodity."

The venerable Gene Sarazen said, "All the professionals should say a silent thanks to Walter Hagen each time they stretch a check between their fingers."

A Hall of Famer with many, many tournament victories on his resume, a man who helped make professional golf respectable, Hagen was also a character who loved a good time. He dressed in dashing, colorful golf outfits and is credited with originating the phrase, "You've got to stop and smell the roses." (Specifically, "Don't hurry. Don't worry. You're only here for a short visit. So don't forget to stop and smell the roses.") Also, he said he didn't want to be a millionaire, he just wanted to live like one. He did eventually amass more than a million dollars in earnings in his career, one of the first sportsmen to do so, although this was earned more from wagering and playing exhibition matches than from tournament prize money.

And there are a few stories that portray his capricious side. On one occasion he was paired with another golfer in a best-of-two-balls format. After carousing all night long, he showed up on the first tee still wearing his tuxedo. He then apologized to his partner for being late and proceeded to pick up his ball on the first five holes, lightheartedly quipping that his partner was carrying him. At that point he caught fire and played so well that his team won the round. On the next day he showed up on time, and in appropriate clothing. They lost that round, however, prompting his partner to say he wished Walter had showed up in a tuxedo again.

Perhaps the story that best illustrates Hagen's impertinent attitude was as follows: It seems that Hagen was invited to play at a private club. He was holding court before teeing off and casually asked what the course record was. When he was told, he claimed that he could break it.

"But you haven't even seen the course yet," someone responded.

"Any takers?" Hagen asked, prompting several members to put up a significant sum against him.

The gallery of bettors followed him around the course as he entertained them with his trademark stream of chatter and good-humored wisecracks. Finally he came to number eighteen where he faced a curling 12-foot putt to break the record. With so much money on the line, the spectators could scarcely breathe. But Hagen casually stepped up to the ball, tapped it toward the hole, then actually turned his back and began to walk away. As the ball was still rolling, he barked, "Pay up, suckers!" and then experienced the satisfaction of hearing the ball go kerplunk in the hole.

Walter Hagen racked up forty-four tour victories and commanded respect among both his professional peers and golf's upper-crust country club set. He also captained the first six Ryder Cup teams in addition to playing on the first five. But his legacy also includes a personality that could light up an entire golf course. In addition to his golfing excellence, he made the game fun. And for us amateurs, at least, that's what it's supposed to be all about.

Arnie's Army
Arnold Palmer, US Open

If there's one golfer who popularized the game more than any other, it was surely Arnold Daniel Palmer. Arnie comes from the Western Pennsylvania town of Latrobe, where he was born September 10, 1929. His father, Deacon, was the greenskeeper and head professional at the Latrobe Country Club, and young Arnie was his dad's prize student. And in addition to golf, he inherited his father's work ethic and common touch, a characteristic that would ultimately endear him to millions who had come from similar circumstances.

As his game continued to flourish, Palmer eventually entered Wake Forest University on a golf scholarship. But when his close friend Bud Worsham passed away, a distraught Palmer left the university and entered the Coast Guard. He didn't abandon golf, however. While in the service he managed to hone his skills, and after three years he returned to school and picked up where he had left off.

Palmer won the US Amateur in 1954, after which he and his new bride, Winifred Walzer, made the joint decision for him to move up to the professional level. And the man who would eventually be known as "The King" would find immediate success. In his first year on tour in 1955, Palmer established himself as a force to be reckoned with by winning The Canadian Open. And three years later he would secure his first major victory at the 1958 Masters tournament.

In 1960 he secured his second Masters title, and although it may not have been apparent at the moment, Arnie and his legion of followers, aptly named "Arnie's Army," were embarking on a journey that by year's end would take on epic proportions.

As Palmer made his way to the 1960 US Open at Cherry Hills, he was clearly considered one of the favorites, but the tournament did not start as he had hoped. In fact, his quest for his first US Open title had a horrific beginning, as his drive on the very first hole found the stream to the right of the fairway. This inauspicious beginning led to a double bogey six, but he still managed to come back with a round of 72. Not bad for a US Open course, but this left him four shots off the lead. And after a second-round score of 71, he had fallen to a staggering eight shots back.

Now came the final two rounds, which in the 1960 Open were played on the same day, a tradition known as "Open Saturday." Although Palmer continued to scratch and claw, his third round ended with another 72. At that point he found himself in fifteenth place with legends like Ben Hogan and Sam Snead between him and the title. Even a top-ten finish would be an uphill climb.

As Arnie contemplated his precarious situation with reporter Bob Drum of the *Pittsburgh Press,* he asked Drum what would happen if by some miracle he was able to shoot a final round of 65.

Drum responded, "Nothing. You're too far back."

But the brash Palmer wouldn't give up hope and rebutted, "Well, it would give me a 280. Doesn't 280 always win the Open?"

At 1:45 p.m. Arnie began his final round seven shots off the lead, but apparently he was undeterred, starting off on a streak that would make history. On the par four first he came away with a birdie. He followed that with three more birdies, a par on five, and then birdies again on six and seven. Incredibly, he had birdied six of the first seven holes at the notoriously difficult US Open!

Now that he was back in contention, spectators would witness a scene they would be talking about for years to come. As the tournament came to a climax, Arnie's companions vying for the lead included the legendary Ben Hogan, who was desperately seeking a fifth US Open at the twilight of his career, and also the brilliant amateur Jack Nicklaus, who yearned to establish himself among the golfing elite. Meanwhile Palmer was vying to become only the third man to win a Masters and US Open in the same year.

Nicklaus would falter first and fall out of contention. And then, on the par five seventeenth, Hogan went for broke as he tried to reach the green in two. It was not to be. His ball found the water, leading to a disastrous bogey. Undoubtedly distressed, Hogan triple bogeyed the final hole while Palmer scored par on seventeen and eighteen to finish the round with his predicted 65, thus fashioning one of the greatest comebacks in the history of The US Open.

Due in large part to his miraculous victory at Cherry Hills, Arnold Palmer was named the *Sports Illustrated* Sportsman of the Year in 1960. In addition to his winning personality and connection to the common man, that sensational win at Cherry Hills was one of the factors that led to the legions of fans who made up Arnie's Army, and gave the game of golf in America an injection of passion that endures to this day.

Eighty-Two!

Sam Snead, Greater Greensboro Open

The talented Sammy Snead was nothing if not prolific. From the very start he was a winner, and his success rarely wavered during a lifetime of competitive golf. After a victory in West Virginia in 1936, Snead entered his first full season as a professional in 1937 and incredibly won five PGA events in that rookie year. Not one to rest on his laurels, the self-taught golfer went on to win an impressive eight tournaments the very next year, including his first Greater Greensboro Open. After three PGA victories in 1939, three more in 1940, and six in 1941, Snead most likely needed a second house just to hold all of his trophies. But even with all of his success to date, Sam had yet to capture a major victory. Well, that was about to change.

In 1942 he captured the PGA Championship for his first major title. But Slammin' Sammy was far from done. As the years progressed he continued to rack up win after win. From 1936 through 1961 he won eighty-one PGA Tour events, which included three PGA Championships (1942, 1949, and 1951), three Masters titles (1949, 1952, and 1954), and an Open Championship in 1946. Yet after his eighty-first victory at the Tournament of Champions in 1961, it appeared that Snead's impressive run of tournament victories had finally come to an end. From 1962 through 1964 Sam went winless. Now that he had reached the age of fifty plus, most followers of the game accepted the idea that Snead would have to step aside for the younger pros. And that thinking certainly made sense, but Sam knew his fire was still burning, and sure enough the unthinkable occurred.

At the 1965 Greater Greensboro Open, fifty-two-year-old Sam Snead defied Father Time by winning the tournament for the eighth time, and his record eighty-second PGA Tour victory! And as this book goes to press, Tiger Woods is trying to catch him, but Snead still holds the record for the most PGA victories nearly a half century later.

To this day, when the name of Slammin' Sammy Snead is mentioned, golf historians still shake their heads in disbelief about the improbable eighty-two PGA victories garnered by the once-poor boy from Virginia. In case you didn't notice, however, with all of those victories Sam Snead never won a US Open.

The Master of The Masters

Jack Nicklaus, The Masters

The star-studded lineup at the 1965 Masters included names that are known to even the most casual golfer, namely the "Big Three" of Gary Player, Arnold Palmer, and Jack Nicklaus. This trio was larger than life in those days, and head and shoulders above the rest of the field. They still had to contend with each other for coveted major victories, however, and there was no tournament each wanted to win more desperately than the highly venerated Masters.

A year earlier, in 1964, Arnold Palmer took home the green jacket by a solid six strokes over Jack Nicklaus and Dave Marr, thus securing Palmer's grip atop the golfing world. But his reign as "The King" of Augusta wouldn't last for long.

As the '65 Masters got under way, all eyes were on the three favorites. After the first round, Gary Player's score of 66 left him with a tenuous lead over his two rivals. A day later, The Big Three would be tied at the top of the leader board. As they entered the weekend the sports world was anticipating a fight to the finish. But sometimes even the most obvious predictions don't come to fruition, and Jack Nicklaus would see to it that this tournament would be determined well before the final hole.

After Nicklaus tinkered with his putting stroke, he came out in the third round like a man on a mission. His adjustment appeared to be just what the doctor ordered as he sank difficult putts on the second, third, fourth, and sixth. His momentum was building, and soon there was more. He went on to birdie seven and eight, and after adding three more birdies on the back nine, Nicklaus ended the third round with a stunning 64. Not only did that score tie the course record, which was established by Lloyd Mangrum all the way back in 1940, but now Nicklaus had a commanding five-shot lead over Player, and was a nearly insurmountable eight ahead of Palmer.

Now history was truly on the line. Not only was a Masters title at stake, but Ben Hogan's tournament record of 274 was also in Nicklaus's sights. And The Golden Bear would not disappoint. Nicklaus played yet another strong round, closing with a 69, and in doing so he smashed Hogan's record by three strokes with a 271 total. Furthermore, his nine-stroke margin of victory over Player and Palmer was a record as well. But most importantly to Nicklaus, he was the Masters Champion for a second time, and he could look forward to the honor of defending his title the following year.

Perhaps most impressive of all, Nicklaus was still in his mid-twenties. Compared to Player and Palmer, he was just a kid. His future was limitless, the world was his oyster. And if anything, the predictions of his ultimate greatness were far too conservative. Even with the superlatives afforded to the immensely talented Tiger Woods and a number of other young comers who are currently compiling their own collections of trophies, no one has yet mounted a pressing challenge to Nicklaus's collection of major victories. And when it comes to The Masters, the image that still comes to mind is of The Golden Bear donning that coveted green jacket year after year.

Jack Nicklaus and The Masters: intertwined icons that will endure through the history and lore of golf!

Rubber Snake

Lee Trevino, Jack Nicklaus, US Open

The US Open has been the subject of many unusual stories in this collection, and the following madcap incident is no exception. This one occurred at the 1971 Open at the famed Merion Golf Course, and the tournament is remembered as much for the zany antics of the larger-than-life Lee Trevino as for the marvelous play of the competitors.

As the tournament reached the seventy-second and final hole, it was still anyone's title to claim. At least four golfers were in contention. Lee Trevino had a golden chance for victory but missed a makeable 6-footer for par. Nicklaus also had an outside chance for the win but missed a 15-foot birdie attempt. The amateur, Jim Simmons, would have been a part of the playoff if he could have ended with a birdie, but after his drive he found the rough and was eliminated with a double bogey. And lastly, Bob Rosburg, the 1959 PGA Championship title holder, needed a final birdie to join Trevino and Nicklaus in the playoff, but he also failed as his putter let him down and he limped to the finish with a three-putt for bogey.

Hence, the scene was set for a Monday eighteen-hole playoff between Lee Trevino and Jack Nicklaus. One on one. *Mano a mano*. As the combatants arrived for the playoff, the tension had built to fever pitch. They stood on the first tee, just minutes away from teeing off, when in the midst of an anxious moment, Trevino pulled a rubber snake out of his bag and playfully tossed it at Nicklaus. As legend has it, Jack jumped a couple feet in the air and was momentarily rattled. But in reality Jack saw it coming, and both men, and the gallery, all had a good laugh and the tension was lifted ... if just for a moment.

As the playoff got under way, Jack started off strong with a birdie on the first hole, but that situation quickly changed as a couple of nasty sand traps would be his early undoing.

On both the second and third holes Nicklaus failed on his first attempt at getting his shots out of the bunker, resulting in a two-shot advantage for Trevino. And although Jack was able to cut the lead back to a single shot on more than one occasion, it seemed that Lee somehow always had the answer to Jack's charge. Case in point, Nicklaus birdied the fifth and Trevino came back three holes later with a birdie on the eighth. Then, after the turn when Jack birdied the eleventh, Lee came right back and birdied twelve. And when Nicklaus was making an eleventh-hour charge on the fifteenth with a makeable birdie putt within his grasp, Trevino struck first by sinking a longer birdie putt of his own.

At this point, Nicklaus all but conceded defeat. The outcome was no longer in doubt, the remaining holes just an anticlimax to the earlier fireworks. Trevino had done it! In capturing his second US Open, Lee Trevino had once again put his stamp on immortality. But despite his great performance and courage under fire, the 1971 US Open is remembered as much for Trevino's hilarious "rubber snake attack" as for his incredible playoff victory over one of golf's most venerable legends.

Throughout his career, Trevino has jabbered and joked his way through virtually every round. His antics have delighted thousands upon thousands of spectators, and if anyone doubts that laughter is the best medicine, they have only to look at his overflowing trophy case. Lee certainly had the goods when it came to playing the game, but like very few others, he was able to do so while maintaining an infectious grin and a skip in his step. With his remarkable talent and loveable personality, it's no wonder that the Merry Mex is still remembered as one of the most beloved pros in in the history of the game.

Forty-Footer

Jack Nicklaus, The Masters

In the mid-1970s Jack Nicklaus was golf's shining star. As he entered the '75 Masters tournament, he already had four green jackets in his closet, plus eight additional major championships for a total of a tidy dozen. But like any true champion, Nicklaus was hungry for more. And the world's dominant player did not disappoint.

Jack came out of the chute like a thoroughbred, shooting under par by posting a 68 for day one, which left him just a single shot off the lead. Bolstered by his fast start, he kept the momentum rolling with an even better round on day two, a 67.

Nicklaus was now six strokes clear of Tom Weiskopf and a formidable eleven ahead of the talented Johnny Miller. At this point the smart money was on Jack to win his fifth green jacket, but even the lowliest hacker can attest to how capricious and cruel this beautiful game can be, how the rug can be pulled out from under one's feet without a moment's notice, and even the world's best golfer was no exception.

Although Jack must have been confident going into his third round, his normally solid game suddenly deserted him, causing him to struggle to the finish with an over par, lackluster 73. Meanwhile, during the same round his two main threats, Weiskopf and Miller, were making their moves, putting up sizzling scores of 66 and 65, respectively. And just like that, Nicklaus was down one shot off

Weiskopf's lead, with the talented Johnny Miller on Jack's tail just three shots back. It was still anyone's tournament as the three competitors entered Sunday's final round.

The competition got even tighter during the front nine, so that at the turn Nicklaus and Weiskopf were tied for the lead with Miller in striking distance only two shots behind. The slightest miscue could change everything, and sure enough, Weiskopf found the water on hole eleven and Miller missed a couple of very makeable putts. The door had opened a generous crack for Nicklaus, but the outcome was still in doubt.

Now the scene was set at green number sixteen where Nicklaus faced a challenging 40-foot putt, while Weiskopf and Miller watched from the tee. As usual Jack was methodical, eyeing every possible angle and green fluctuation. Most observers felt that it was a challenge for him to save par by two-putting, whereas even a three-putt was a distinct possibility. But Jack remained unflappable. He lined up his putt and remained icy calm as he made his usual silky stroke.

The crowd held its breath as Jack's ball tracked toward the hole, then erupted into jubilation as the little white sphere found the bottom of the cup. Nicklaus ended the round with a 68, a score that might be good enough to win, but it wasn't over yet. His opponents were still on the course and still in contention, so Jack had to cool his heels in the clubhouse, totally at the mercy of fortune and destiny. With the drama that only a major championship can provide, both Miller and Weiskopf could force a playoff by scoring a birdie on the seventy-second hole. And as fate would have it, each man set himself up for a tying birdie putt. And they gave it their all, but neither one was able to find the cup, resulting in Miller and Weiskopf sharing a two-way tie for second.

In the end it would be Jack's incredible 40-foot birdie putt on sixteen that gave him the one-stroke margin of victory and his record fifth green jacket. Television cameras recorded his moment of golfing glory in Butler Cabin, and Jack graciously accepted the attention. But even at that moment, The Golden Bear must have been dreaming of the future because he certainly wasn't done making history at Augusta National. There was more to come. Lots more.

Pump Up the Volume

Tiger Woods,
TPC Scottsdale Tournament

Golf has traditionally been a sport for the refined elite. In accordance with the example inherited from the British Isles, even spectators have generally understood that they are to appear in the proper attire, adhere strictly to the etiquette of the game, and express approval of a player's performance with a restrained dignity. Applause is to be bestowed by gently and appropriately tapping one's hands in appreciation of a job well done. It mustn't be too loud, boisterous, or in any way offensive to the eardrum. Heavens no! Not too much, not too little.

But somewhere around the turn of the twenty-first century, a perceptible shift began to take place. The rules of decorum yielded to expressions of emotion, and in this author's humble opinion, the accompanying impertinent attitude has made golf even more enjoyable than it was previously. Nowhere is this raucous behavior more evident than at the TPC Scottsdale Tournament in Arizona.

The TPC Scottsdale is widely appreciated as a terrific tournament. Big prize money, excellent weather, and an *enthusiastic* crowd. Okay, to be honest, the place is more like a boozed-up frat party that just happens to be taking place at a golfing event. This carnival-like atmosphere is most notable at hole number sixteen, the 162-yard par three aptly known as "The Coliseum" or "the loudest hole in golf."

Ironically, the tranquil pink and purple McDowell Mountain Range acts as a majestic backdrop, a scene that might impose awe-inspired silence to an appreciative observer, but the putting green is encompassed by a 20,000-seat stadium that packs in the rowdiest crowd golf has ever known. If a golfer should falter, he will surely hear the taunting and jeers of the merciless herd. However, if a player finds the magic touch, the 20,000 faithful will show their approval with, uh, unrestrained exuberance.

For evidence, I refer you to the 1997 tournament where a newcomer to the sport, Tiger Woods, was in his second season on tour. Tiger had made a huge splash that year by winning his first Masters in historic fashion, and was already the most popular player on the tour. So when he approached the fabled sixteenth at the Scottsdale TPC, the crowd was geared up and ready to go, and Tiger delivered in grand style.

As Woods stood in the tee box, he looked out into the sea of anxious onlookers, adjusted for the wind, grabbed his club, and as usual, put a hurtin' on the ball. The crowd oohed and aahed as it tracked toward the green, and as if drawn by a magnet, Tiger's ball found the bottom of the cup for a hole-in-one! Now, an ace in golf is nothing to sneeze at, especially in a PGA event. But in this case, 20,000 strong went absolutely berserk! Virtually every spectator was in a frenzy. Beer bottles were literally thrown into the air, and the noise level was almost deafening, so much so that Tiger's hole-in-one at the 1997 TPC Scottsdale is largely considered to be "the loudest hole in golf's history."

Tiger Woods has done many miraculous things during his famed golfing career. He has had the highest of highs and the lowest of lows. But in 1997, when he combined his charismatic personality with an improbable hole-in-one in front of a rowdy audience, the result was a roar so loud that it could be heard from miles around, adding another incredible moment to the legend that is the sixteenth hole at the TPC Scottsdale . . . the loudest hole in golf!

(PS: This historic moment can be found on www.youtube.com. Simply enter "the loudest hole in golf," but I would suggest turning down the volume before doing so.)

Wonder Woman

Nancy Marie Lopez, Rookie Dominance

Golf superstars come in many shapes and forms, and from a wide range of backgrounds.

Despite being associated with the trappings of a country club lifestyle, our beloved game has produced any number of individuals who sprang from modest beginnings. A case in point is one Nancy Marie Lopez, who was to become far and away the most dominant name in women's golf.

Nancy was born on January 6, 1957, in Torrance, California, into a working-class family that had to scrape by on her father's wages as an auto mechanic. Yet somehow her parents found the money to finance their only child's golfing career, an investment that would prove to yield very handsome dividends.

A stellar junior career provided the foundation for what was to come. The young Miss Lopez served notice at the age of twelve when she won the New Mexico Women's Amateur title. Three years later, at age fifteen, she won the prestigious US Girl's Junior title, and repeated that performance two years later. And incredibly, in 1975 as an eighteen-year-old amateur, Lopez barely missed out on winning the Women's US Open when she finished tied for second.

At the University of Tulsa, Lopez was named an All-American and the Female Athlete of the Year. After her sophomore season she made the decision to turn professional, and it would be during her first full season on tour in 1978, that she would make history. Playing with the precision and passion that belied her years, Lopez won her first LPGA tournament by claiming the Bent Tree Classic on February 26. Now that she had tasted big-time victory, she was hungry for more and was about to get a bellyful.

Her second career title came at the Sunstar Classic in March, and she had begun a streak unparalleled by any golfer, man or woman, in a rookie year. On May 14 she won the Greater Baltimore Classic. On May 21 she took the title at the Coca-Cola Classic. The very next week saw her claim victory at the Golden Lights Championship in New York. Then, at her next tournament, the LPGA Championship no less, she would be immortalized by taking that title, too. And finally, on June 18, Lopez would win yet again, this time at the Bankers Trust Classic.

In a script that no one would dare to write, Nancy won five consecutive tournaments in her very first full year. And to top it off, she won the Colgate European Open in August and the Colgate Far East Open on November 12. A staggering nine LPGA events. Nine! In her rookie year!

For her 1978 heroics, Lopez was awarded the Vare trophy for the golfer with the lowest scoring average and graced the cover of *Sports Illustrated*. She was also named the LPGA Rookie of the Year, the LPGA Player of the Year, and the Associated Press Female Athlete of the Year . . . truly amazing! This kind of otherworldly success is often accomplished by an intense, hard-nosed individual who commands respect while keeping others at bay. Not so with Nancy, who wore a perpetual smile with a girl-next-door demeanor that inspired legions of adoring fans, men and women alike.

Nancy would go on to win three majors and a total of forty-eight LPGA victories throughout her illustrious career. Her name and picture appeared countless times on the cover of golf magazines and on

TV sports shows. She became well-known internationally, her face as familiar as any figure in the world of sports. All of this culminated in an induction into the Golf Hall of Fame in 1987. Yet it would be her magical rookie season of 1978 when she first took the golfing world by storm, and in doing so wrote a chapter in golf history that is likely never to be duplicated.

Seve

Severiano Ballesteros, British Open

Severiano "Seve" Ballesteros Sota was born on April 9, 1957, in Pedrena, Spain, the youngest of five sons to parents Baldomero Ballesteros Presmanes and Carmen Sota Ocejo. Although one of the sons tragically died in childhood, the other Ballesteros boys all grew up to be professional golfers.

As a youth, instead of attending school, Seve opted to play golf on the beaches near his home. He was a quick study, though, and the golfing education he received served him well. So well in fact that in March 1974 he turned professional at the age of sixteen. A number of pundits opined that as an adolescent in his mid-teens, Ballesteros was far too young to hang with the big boys. But only a few short years later, in 1976, the highly improbable was occurring. At the Royal Birkdale Golf Club, a nineteen-year-old Seve actually held a two-stroke, fifty-four-hole lead at The British Open. And although he would falter on the final day, he had clearly asserted himself as a force to be reckoned with. In fact, despite that lackluster performance on the last day of the Open, that same nineteen-year-old would go on to claim the European Tour Order of Merit (money title) in that same year. When he was nineteen years old!

As Seve entered the 1979 British Open, he already had several years of professional competition under his belt. Despite his experience, many considered this young pup too raw to make a major championship breakthrough. However the youthful but confident Señor Ballesteros had no such doubts.

In the first round, Seve shot a 73, an acceptable round but not exactly what he had in mind, especially when you consider that Bill Longmuir set the bar with a 65 and the formidable Hale Irwin posted a first round of 68. Seve was well off the lead, but he knew there was still plenty of golf to be played.

On day two, Ballesteros came out *en fuego*! Every shot seemed magical, and when the day was over he was able to sit back and enjoy his round of 65. Now just two shots behind the leader Hale Irwin, Ballesteros knew that he was in striking distance going into the weekend.

Seve's third round saw him take a step back with another lack-luster performance, scoring 75. Luckily for him, though, Irwin also shot a 75, keeping Ballesteros two shots off the lead. However, this left the door open for a couple of formidable contenders, namely Ben Crenshaw and Jack Nicklaus, who were now lurking close behind.

The tension was palpable as the championship came down to the final round. Hale Irwin succumbed by shooting a disappointing 78 to wind up in sixth place. But with Crenshaw and Nicklaus playing solid golf, Seve knew that he would have to perform at his highest level in order to secure his first major title. The bad news was that his driver completely let him down. He had used the big club on nine holes during the final round and missed the fairway on eight out of the nine attempts. The good news was that this creative, imaginative player was able to hack his way out of trouble time and time again. The most amazing example of this Houdini act occurred at the sixteenth hole when Seve actually hit his drive into a parking lot, yet ended the hole with a birdie! At the end of the day he posted a score of 70, good enough to lay claim to the Open title. Years later, as Ben Crenshaw recounted the day's events, he was quoted as saying, "Seve played shots I don't even see in my dreams."

Seve would go on to win a total of three British Opens (1979, 1984, and 1988) as well as two Masters titles (1980 and 1983) for a total of five majors. He amassed ninety-one wins in his professional career (including a number of minor European tournaments that were not official PGA events) and was inducted into the Golf Hall of Fame in 1999.

Sadly, Seve Ballesteros would eventually succumb to a brain tumor, passing away on May 7, 2011, at the age of fifty-four. But it was Seve's winning personality and indomitable spirit that will forever define the man, and his magical performance at the 1979 Open Championship that the golfing world will remember for generations to come.

Ryder Cup Comeback

Ben Crenshaw, Ryder Cup

Most golfers know that the Ryder Cup is an international competition held every two years between golfing teams from the United States and Europe. But what most golfers might not know is that the first Ryder Cup event occurred way back in 1927 at the Worcester Country Club in Worcester, Massachusetts. And the reason it's called the Ryder Cup is that the cup itself was originally donated by a gentleman by the name of Samuel Ryder.

Another thing some golfers don't know is that, win or lose, the players in the Ryder Cup receive no compensation. Despite the fact that this competition has become one of the most highly anticipated contests in sports and generates millions of dollars, there is no prize money. In a refreshing display of patriotism and love for the game of golf, the competitors' prize is simply the honor of being awarded the cup and maintaining possession until being challenged again two years later.

There have been many memorable Ryder Cup events over nearly a century of play, but the 1999 contest at the Brookline Country Club was truly one to remember. Through the first two days of competition the Europeans were dominating, and if history was any indicator, it was all but over. The Europeans had a commanding 10–6 advantage, and no team had ever come back from more than two points down on the final day. In actuality, the Europeans would only need four points to retain the title. Yet the American team captain, Ben Crenshaw, never gave up hope, stating repeatedly that he believed in fate and that the US team would ultimately prevail.

As the Americans began the singles matches, the improbable began to occur. Incredibly, the stateside boys won the first six matches in dominant fashion, closing out each and every victory before the seventeenth hole. Now with the Americans back in the thick of things, the two teams would fight tooth and nail to the finish.

With the outcome very much in doubt, it all came down to Justin Leonard's matchup with Jose Maria Olazabal. The good news for the Americans was that Leonard would only need to halve the contest to ensure a US victory. The bad news was that Justin had never won a Ryder Cup match and was all but dead, four holes down with seven to play.

But Leonard wouldn't quit. In a stunning display of determination and skill, Justin won four straight holes to even the match, and by the time he and Olazabal approached the seventeenth green, the match was all square. Leonard addressed his 45-foot birdie putt while 30,000 astonished fans watched in frozen anticipation. He studied the break carefully, took his position over the ball, stroked it with precision, and *voila!*, the ball fell squarely into the cup as the crowd roared its approval. The shaken Olazabal had a chance to halve the hole with a putt of his own, but it was not to be. With one hole to play, Leonard was assured of at least a tie. The Ryder Cup would be coming back to America.

In the end, the United States won 8½ points on the final day of competition to post a 14½ to 13½ final victory. It had taken a near miracle, and after the greatest comeback victory in the history of the Ryder Cup, a choked-up Captain Crenshaw was quoted as saying, "I never stopped believing. I'm stunned. This is so indescribable."

The Magic Number

Annika Sorenstam, Standard Register Ping

There are certain magical numbers in sports: the 4-minute mile in track and field; the perfect 300 in bowling; the .400 batting average in baseball; and in golf, the highly coveted score of 59, a score of *thirteen under par* for the standard seventy-two-hole golf course. While this magical mark has been reached precious few times on the men's professional circuit, going into the 2001 season no woman had managed to do so on the LPGA Tour. Ah, but read on ...

Annika Sorenstam was born in Bro, Sweden, on October 9, 1970. As a child, Annika was an exceptional all-around athlete, reaching a national ranking in junior tennis. She also excelled in soccer and skiing, but at age twelve she decided to focus on golf, a momentous decision that was destined to change the face of the sport as well as the perception of women as athletes.

With an enormous talent matched by an equally strong work ethic, Sorenstam's game developed quickly. A stellar junior career followed, and she was soon spotted by a coach from the United States. This led to a notable college career at the University of Arizona, including an NCAA individual golf championship. Then, in 1992, Sorenstam made the decision to turn professional.

Her pro career was actually a bit rocky in the beginning. She didn't score a single win for the first three years. But when she finally did enter the winner's circle, she did it with a flourish, taking nothing less than the US Women's Open title in 1995. This grand entrance into golf's stratosphere opened the floodgates, and Sorenstam never looked back. By the end of the 1990s Sorenstam had racked up more titles than any other LPGA competitor during the decade.

Having accomplished so many lofty goals at such a young age, Sorenstam admitted that she temporarily lost her focus, allowing Karri Webb to take over the number one ranking.

At that point Sorenstam went back to work, embarking on an intensive workout program that got her into the best shape of her life. Now she was ready to dominate the sport once again.

During the 2001 season, she was back on track, racking up eight LPGA titles by season's end. The real excitement, however, occurred during that year's Standard Register Ping event.

To set the scene, Sorenstam began her second round on the back nine. The day started off well with a birdie on the tenth. It got a little bit better with another birdie on the eleventh. And then another on the twelfth. And the thirteenth! And the fourteenth! All the way through number seventeen!

Are you counting? That made eight straight holes with a birdie! Eight under par after eight holes! She "faltered" a bit on hole number eighteen, managing to make only a meager par, but then she got back on the birdie train, scoring four more in a row. Still counting? That's twelve under through thirteen holes!

As word spread around the course, the patrons flocked to get a glimpse of history in the making. The magical round continued until Sorenstam approached the final hole. After a successful drive she placed her approach shot 10 feet above the hole and needed only to two-putt for history. And after tapping in her final putt she leapt into the arms of her caddie, Terry McNamara. Sorenstam had done it! Thirteen birdies, no bogeys, and twenty-five stingy putts on the 6,459-yard course, and never encountering a par putt longer than 3½ feet. Anika Sorenstam thus became the first woman to ever shoot a 59 in a professional event, besting the previous record of 61, which she shared with Karri Webb and Se Ri Pak. After the round Sorenstam would say, "I made such an incredible start, and it was such fun, to put it mildly. By the end I started to get very nervous. But now I'm so proud and happy."

Anika Sorenstam retired at the end of the 2008 season with seventy-two official LPGA tournament victories and ten major titles. By this time she had already been inducted into the Golf Hall of Fame (in 2003), and as this book goes to print she remains the only woman golfer to ever shoot a sub-60 round on the LGPA tour . . . truly amazing!

US Open Dominance

Tiger Woods, US Open

The US Open is generally acknowledged as one of the most difficult tests a golfer can face. Played on the most difficult courses, with narrow fairways, deep roughs, and lightning-fast greens, it is a near certainty that any player who manages to finish with a score anywhere near par will be in the hunt for the title.

As we all know now, Tiger Woods has clearly established himself as one of the all-time giants of the game. But back in 2000, as he entered the US Open, his professional greatness was yet to be determined. Granted, he had a magical run at the 1997 Masters. And he also took the 1999 PGA Championship with a nail-biting, one-stroke victory over Sergio Garcia. And yes, I admit that two major titles in one's back pocket isn't anything to sneeze at. But let's face facts. In 2000 the jury was still out. Would Tiger Woods be another flash in the pan who would end up as a footnote for having taken a couple of big trophies and then disappear? Or would time prove that he would he go down as one of the true legends of the sport?

As Woods began his first round at Pebble Beach, he had, well, "the eye of the tiger." And after a masterful score of 65, he held a one-shot advantage over the field. Then on day two he came right back with a solidly constructed 69. So after thirty-six holes he had posted a total of 134, giving him a commanding six-stroke lead over the field as he entered the weekend.

Tiger was still a youngster at the time, but he had experienced enough high-level competition to know that anything could happen. A moment or two of losing one's focus, especially at a US Open, and a lead can disappear in a heartbeat. His father had hammered this home to him a thousand times, so he wasn't about to take his foot off the gas. After a solid third round score of 71, he now had a virtually insurmountable ten-stroke advantage. Now all that was left was to see if the kid from California could make history.

Even in 2000, Woods was clearly one of the most popular players on tour. Not surprisingly, he had a huge gallery following him and millions more rooting for him from their televisions at home. So what happened on the Sunday final? I think it would be fair to call it a slam dunk. Tiger shot yet another masterful round, posting a 67, and when all of the scorecards were signed, the true magnitude of the victory began to take shape.

Tiger Woods had tallied a four-day total score of 272, incredible for a US Open. But the enormity of his victory becomes apparent when one considers the following statistics: The winning margin was fifteen strokes; he was the only player to score under par; and his final score was twelve under, meaning that his closest rival was three over par for the tournament, a score that has been good enough to claim the title in previous Opens.

Tiger's win at the US Open that year is hands down one of most dominating performances in the history of major championship golf. And when one takes into account the difficulty of a US Open course, the multitude of talented players from around the globe, and Tiger's incredible margin of victory, his accomplishment raised the bar to a level that might well be permanently unreachable.

Long John

John Patrick Daly, PGA Championship

If the reader will indulge this humble author in a classic understatement, John Patrick Daly is not exactly whom one would call a conventional golfer. Born on April 28, 1966, in Carmichael, California, John moved with his family to Dardanelle, Arkansas, when he was just four years old. At age five he picked up the game that would one day make him famous, and from then on he paid very little attention to the "established" rules. On the contrary, as John grew up he became a fiery, beer-guzzling, football-playing young man who just happened to be an excellent golfer. His talents on the links proved so prolific that he eventually ended up on the University of Arkansas golf team. And although he would leave the school before graduating, his time in college laid the foundation for his golfing prowess to flourish.

He subsequently turned professional in 1987, finding immediate success with a victory that same year at the Missouri Open. Although the Missouri win was not a sanctioned PGA Tour event, it still gave Daly an infusion of cash as well as the confidence to move his career forward. After a few more non-PGA victories, he continued to grind it out while hoping for the opportunity to make a big splash. And in 1991, just such an opportunity presented itself.

Daly was the ninth alternate for the PGA Championship in 1991. There were eight people in line ahead of him, yet as fate would have it, when Nick Price had to drop out of the tournament at the eleventh hour because his wife was about to have a baby, no other alternate could make it to the event in time. Daly didn't hesitate. He grabbed the chance of a lifetime, driving all night from his home in Memphis to make his tee time for the first round in Carmel, Indiana.

The tournament was held at the Crooked Stick Golf Club. Undoubtedly sleep deprived after his overnight journey, Daly stepped right onto the very long, very difficult golf course, which, by the way, he had never seen, and conquered it with an opening-round 69. His booming drives wowed the spectators, and the 7,289-yard track, the second longest in the history of the PGA Championships, served him well. Those mammoth drives would soon earn him the nickname "Long John."

But being long off the tee wasn't John's only talent. His iron play and putting proved to be equally solid, leading to a second-round score of an even more impressive 67. Now he was atop the leader board, and the golfing world started to take notice.

He maintained his remarkable pace by shooting another 69 in round three, his third straight sub-70 performance. As he entered the final round, again with the lead, he surely must have been nervous about reaching for his first big win, but if he was shaking in his boots, he didn't show it. Once again he played a solid round, this time posting a score of 71.

Incredibly, "Long John" Daly had done what seemed impossible just days earlier. With twenty-one birdies and one eagle, the no-name ninth alternate became the first rookie on the PGA tour to win a major tournament since Jerry Pate took the US Open in 1976. His four-day total score was an impressive twelve-under-par 276, earning him the title by three stokes. And I'm sure the $230,000 winner's paycheck didn't hurt even a little bit.

John Daly has gone on to have many ups and downs in his career. To date he has won five PGA Tour events, including a second major at the 1995 British Open, where he prevailed in a dramatic playoff. But on the dark side, this take-no-prisoners cowboy has also battled with alcoholism and gambling over the years, and is currently trying to find his way back to the top of the golfing world. Yet despite what happens in John Daly's future, he has already given the golf world a lifetime of memories, none of which was more thrilling than that first improbable victory at the 1991 PGA Championship!

A Day at the Beach

Gary Player,

British Open

How is it that the professionals can make sand shots look so easy while the rest of us hackers struggle so mightily? Yet even among the experts there are many degrees of beach aptitude. Some routinely get up and down with no apparent effort, while others look like they're digging for buried treasure.

When it comes to The British Open, the sand traps are a different animal, more like meteor craters in the middle of the golf course, some of them deeper than a tall man. We've all seen some of the world's best get humiliated by those devilishly designed abysses, but when it comes to getting out of the grain there's one player who is considered perhaps the best ever. And that player is none other than "The Black Knight," Gary Player.

Gary Player was born on November 1, 1935, in Johannesburg, South Africa. The youngest of three children, his mother tragically died of cancer when he was eight years old. His father worked in the gold mines to support the family, and though money was tight, Mr. Player was able to secure a loan in order to purchase young Gary his first set of clubs. Gary immediately fell in love with the game and played whenever he had the chance. His proficiency seemed to improve on a daily basis, so much so that he was able to turn professional at seventeen years of age.

As his record clearly illustrates, Gary Player would prove to be one of the best golfers to ever play the game. He has won a mind-numbing 165 tournaments on six continents over six decades, racking up some improbable frequent flyer credits as he's traveled over 15 million miles during his career. He has become so popular that there is very little that we still don't know about this living legend. But here's a story you may not have heard . . .

In 1990, at the age of fifty-four, Player was still fighting it out with the young guns on the PGA Tour. And while the 1990 British Open is widely remembered for Nick Faldo's impressive five-stroke victory, a performance that went under the radar was Player's Houdini sand act.

As he navigated the course at the 119th Open Championship at St. Andrews, Player found quite a few pitfalls in the form of what appeared to be mini deserts. As anyone who has ever watched The British Open can attest, the sand traps are some of the most treacherous in the world. So when his ball strayed into these bottomless pits on nine separate occasions, even The Black Knight, who was largely regarded as one of the best sand players in the world, must have thought he was on a different planet. To most of us, this would have been a nightmare. But incredibly, Player got up and down on eight of the nine holes. And in case you're thinking he must have failed on the ninth, think again. He holed that one out!

There's a joke about a guy who tells his new golf partner that he has trouble getting out of sand traps. But when he encounters his first one he takes a beautiful smooth swing with his sand wedge, pops the ball out gracefully, and it checks up with impressive backspin a few inches from the hole. His playing partner was astonished. "I thought you said you can't get out of sand traps!" he said. Upon which the guy in the trap beckoned with an outstretched arm and pleaded, "I can't. Please pull me out of here!"

Needless to say, that guy wasn't Gary Player, one of the fittest players on the tour. No doubt, The Black Knight walked out of every bunker he ever visited with no trouble whatsoever. And he surely walked proudly out of those traps at the 1990 British Open after producing perhaps the finest display of sand performance in the history of professional golf.

Big off the Tee

Carl Cooper, H.E.B. Texas Open

Every professional golfer dreams of qualifying for the PGA Tour. Yet for the lucky few who have the skill, determination, and luck to get there, there are countless others, some literally living in their cars, just hoping to make it to the big time.

Such was the case for Carl Cooper, who grew up with enough talent and ambition to reach for the stars. After a successful career at the University of Houston, he decided to make the leap and turned professional. And in 1990 things looked promising as he made it through the grueling Qualifying School to earn his precious PGA Tour card. He struggled on the tour, however, and returned to "Q" School for the next several years in order to retain his playing privileges.

But finally, in 1992, Cooper's name would go down in the history books. Playing at the H.E.B. Texas Open, Carl came to the 444-yard par four, third hole at the Oak Hill Country Club. He selected his oversize driver, took one last gaze out over the fairway, addressed his ball, and took a mighty swipe. As he would later state, "I tried to cut the ball, and I cut it too much."

As Carl's big, wayward drive veered to the right it eventually landed on a downhill cart path. "It kept bouncing and bouncing and bouncing," he said. After finally finding its way off the cart path, things went from bad to worse. His ball continued to roll on a maintenance path. Cooper would go on to state, "If you and I were playing, we'd never have found the ball. But because it was a tournament, a marshal found [it]." When it finally came to rest, the drive had traveled 331 yards *past the green* for a grand total of 787 yards!

So what came next? Because there were no out-of-bounds markers, Cooper was forced to play his second shot back toward the green. He had to hit a four iron and then an eight iron just to get there, eventually scrambling for a heroic double-bogey six, all this after hitting the longest drive in the history of tournament golf.

Carl Cooper played in ninety-nine events over his career, making just twenty-seven cuts. He had four top twenty-five finishes but never finished in the top ten. His career earnings totaled just $115,317. But Carl can put his head on the pillow every night knowing that he did indeed make history with a booming drive that may never be matched!

PS: In case you were wondering, the longest golf ball ever hit on planet Earth traveled an astonishing 2,640 yards (1½ miles). How is that possible? Nils Lied struck the famed shot in 1962 from Mawson Base, Antarctica, on packed ice.

The Sweet Taste of Victory
David Duval, PGA Tour

For most pros, a PGA victory is the culmination of a lifetime of blood, sweat, and tears. And for a very lucky few, success actually comes in their first few weeks on tour. In most cases, that prized trip to the winner's circle never happens. But there is a third group of golfers, the ones who fight for months, and even years, before finally making his or her major breakthrough, and this scenario is inevitably a glorious spectacle to behold. Watching a determined competitor reach a life-long dream after years of gut-wrenching effort does the heart good. And there is no better example of this than the exceptionally talented David Duval.

David Robert Duval was born on November 9, 1971, in Jacksonville, Florida. The middle child of a golf instructor, young David was born with the game in his bloodline. Not surprisingly he had a very successful amateur career, and after winning the US Junior Amateur Championship during his senior year of high school, he brought his talents to Georgia Tech. As part of the Yellow Jackets' golf team, Duval was a four-time first-team All-American, a two-time Atlantic Coast Conference Player of the Year, and the 1993 National Player of the Year during his senior season. After achieving so much as an amateur, Duval's next logical step was up, this time to the professional ranks.

The Nike Tour was the venue for his first two wins, after which he earned his coveted PGA Tour card in 1995. Now he was poised for a win at the top level, and he came oh so close, finishing in second place a total of seven times. Two years on the tour, eighty-six tournaments, seven second-place finishes, and no titles. To be winless was certainly not uncommon, but because he had just missed on so many occasions, he must have been desperate for that first PGA victory.

Then, on October 12, 1997, at the Michelob Championship at Kingsmill, David found himself in a playoff with Grant Waite and Duffy Waldorf. But this time . . . *finally*, Duval would come through to earn his first PGA title.

Now, dear reader, you must be thinking the following: Nice story, warm and fuzzy and all that, but is this really one of the most memorable moments in golf history? Well, keep reading, because the very next week David found himself in another playoff, this time at the Walt Disney World/Oldsmobile Classic, and once again he prevailed, his second victory in successive weeks. And of course (!), in his very next tournament he won yet again, this time at the prestigious Tour Championship with a one-stroke victory over Jim Furyk.

After going winless in eighty-six straight tournaments, David Duval became the first golfer since Ben Hogan to win his first three PGA Tour titles in consecutive events! And although his streak ended at three, he went on to take ten titles out of thirty-three tournaments, beginning with his October victory at the Michelob Championship.

But as in Newtonian physics, what goes up must come down. After several more years of flying high, including a major title at The British Open in 2001, Duval has come back to earth and has yet to post another win in more than a decade. Even so, the talented Mr. Duval certainly made his mark along the way, and will be remembered for that incandescent stretch when he had his first taste of victory, and then came right back for seconds . . . and thirds!

True Greatness

Jack Nicklaus, Decades of Excellence

Making a living on the links is a truly remarkable achievement. As for those who are able to win a professional tournament, they earn the respect of their peers and adoring fans. And as for those few who are able to win a major championship, well, they are enshrined into the hallowed history books of golfing lore. But to be one of the *greats,* to go down as one of the best who have ever played the game, to reach the pinnacle of the sport, you have to win again, and again, and again.

Although it is the subject of many an intense discussion, Jack Nicklaus is largely considered to be the greatest who has ever played the game. And while many simply look at his eighteen majors as proof, I would offer the following: One could argue that to be considered the greatest of the great, you not only need to win tournaments, but they need to be major tournaments, and you need to consistently be at the top of the game. In other words, there are no flash-in-the-pans. The legends are always there, always challenging for the titles. And even if they're not winning, they are always in contention to the end. Still need proof of Nicklaus's greatness? Consider this:

As previously mentioned, Jack has won an astonishing, record-setting eighteen majors. But what most observers of the sport don't realize is that "The Golden Bear" has finished in the top four in major championships an incredible *fifty-four* times. It started in 1960, when he finished second to Arnold Palmer at The US Open. And it ended in 1986 when he miraculously won The Masters. All in all, Jack played in 100 majors and finished in the top four an astonishing 54 percent of the time. And in case you're still not convinced, in Nicklaus's prime, from 1962 to 1980, he placed in the top four in major championships on forty-seven separate occasions—61.8 percent of the time!

One can make the case for many golfers as the best who have ever played the game. With apologies in advance to those deserving candidates I have not included, I would offer the following names, every one iconic, every one synonymous with the sport of golf:

Walter Hagen, Gene Sarazen, Bobby Jones, Tommy Armour, Sam Snead, Ben Hogan, Arnold Palmer, Gary Player, Byron Nelson, Billy Casper, Lee Trevino, Tom Watson, Seve Ballasteros, Tiger Woods, and in this author's opinion, the most purely talented, without regard to records or single-minded devotion to the game, Phil Mickelson. And of course there are the current luminaries, some of whom will also leave their mark.

But if one is going to use consistency as a benchmark, no one, *but no one*—including the spectacular Tiger Woods—has come close to the record of Jack Nicklaus. So until someone comes along with stats that pose a legitimate challenge, the heavyweight title "The Greatest Ever" goes to none other than Mister Consistency, The Golden Bear, Jack William Nicklaus.

Temper, Temper

Brian Barnes, French Open

The French might call it *savoir faire*. The British strive to keep a stiff upper lip. In American slang it's "keeping your cool." Whatever the culture, it's easier said than done when it comes to maintaining control over one's emotions, especially in the midst of a frustrating round on the links.

Brian Barnes was born on June 3, 1945, in Addington, Surrey, England. As a youngster, Brian was taught to play golf by his father, who was the secretary at Burnham and Berrow Golf Clubs. Barnes was a fine pupil and would later turn professional in 1964. And by all accounts he had quite a successful career. He was one of the European Tour's best golfers in the 1970s and won nine events between 1972 and 1981. Not to mention that he made a nice living along the way, finishing between fourth and eighth on the Order of Merit (money list) every year from 1971 to 1980. Plus, he is widely remembered for beating Jack Nicklaus twice during the 1975 Ryder Cup . . . and he did it on the same day!

Ah, but alas, Brian Barnes is also remembered for another day, a day he'd surely rather forget. It happened during the second round of the 1968 French Open at Saint Cloud. Barnes was actually near the top of the leader board when he teed off at the par three eighth hole. Unfortunately, his drive found the bunker, and he followed that up with a poor shot that left him with a long putt for par. When the short-tempered Brit left his putt 3 feet short of the hole, his frustration got the best of him and he began to seethe and swear under his breath. Then it got worse. Now furious, Barnes inexplicably approached his errant putt and attempted to "rake" it in. When his hockey-style maneuver failed, he continued to bat the ball back and forth while it was still moving. Mercifully, the ball eventually found the cup, but when this bizarre display came to an end he had racked up a score of fifteen and subsequently stormed off the course.

After his European Tour playing days were over, Barnes would go on to have a successful professional senior career, most notably winning the Senior British Open in 1995, and the next year he was the first man to successfully defend his title when he won again in 1996. Following several more productive years, arthritis finally got the best of him and he retired from professional golf in 2000.

The talented Mr. Barnes will be remembered for many things. No doubt his trophy case will attest to the fact that he was a superb golfer. But it was an ill-fated day at the 1968 French Open that saw him blow his top, and ended with an historic moment of infamy . . . temper, temper.

"The Shot Heard 'Round the World"

Gene Sarazen, The Masters

This phrase, "the Shot Heard 'Round the World," was originally applied to America's Revolutionary War, describing the proverbial first shot fired in 1775 between British forces and local militia in Lexington, Massachusetts. Since then it has been applied to numerous other situations, including the winning goal by the US hockey team against the Soviets in the 1980 Olympics, and the famous Bobby Thompson home run in 1951 that clinched the pennant for the New York Giants. ("The Giants win the pennant! The Giants win the pennant! The Giants win the pennant! The Giants win the pennant!"—repeated by the announcer *four times*—a surefire stumper in a trivia contest.)

But we're talking about golf here, where this popular phrase refers to an incident in the 1935 Masters Tournament, more specifically a golf shot by a fellow named Sarazen that bordered on the miraculous.

Gene Sarazen was born on February 27, 1902, in Harrison, New York. He was introduced to the game of golf by caddieing, then learned how to play by his own wits. Interestingly, he was noted for using an interlocking grip, commonly employed now but an unusual practice at the time. Starting in his mid-teens, Gene worked as a golf pro at various clubs in the New York area, then had early success as a touring pro, winning the 1922 US Open and the PGA Championships as a young man, just twenty years old.

Along with his contemporaries and arch competitors, Bobby Jones and Walter Hagen, Sarazen had a huge influence in drawing attention to the sport of golf, also establishing the United States as the dominant power in world golf over the previously dominant Great Britain.

Sarazen was a physically small man, standing just over 5 feet 5 inches tall, but he developed a technique for hitting a long ball, thus allowing him to compete with golfers of greater physical stature. He was also an innovator, inventing and designing the first sand wedge by building up a flange that sat lower than the leading edge, allowing for an explosion shot that was accomplished by first hitting the sand behind the ball rather than making direct contact, which was the previously accepted technique.

But what about "the shot heard 'round the world"? Well, that happened in the remote little town of Augusta, Georgia, the site of the relatively young but already revered Masters Tournament. Sarazen was playing on Sunday, in the last round, and trailing the leader, Craig Wood, by three strokes. Then came hole number fifteen, a 485-yard par five known as "Firethorn," where he had just launched his drive a respectable 250 yards onto the fairway, but still a distant 235 yards from the hole. (Keep in mind that in 1935, 485 yards was a respectable distance for a par five. The drivers had wooden heads, not metal, and shafts weren't made of the high-tech fiberglass and graphite technology that adds so much extra yardage to today's monster tee shots.)

Gene Sarazen, our little golfer standing 235 yards from the hole, selected a four wood, put his smooth swing on the ball, and propelled it toward the green . . .

Of all the exceptional shots in golf, most people will tell you the hole-in-one is the rarest, but in fact that designation belongs to the ultra-rare double eagle. This is scored in one of two ways: either a pin-seeking drive on a par four (usually a relatively short hole) or a mammoth clout of a second shot on a par five that has to travel long and straight in order to find the distant hole. Such was the case with Mr. Sarazen's spectacular four wood, which gave him a score of 2 on that par five. With that single stroke he made up the three shots by which he had trailed Craig Wood. They remained tied at the end of regulation play, thus forcing a thirty-six-hole playoff that Sarazen won the next day.

Consider the hapless Craig Wood, to whom the winner's check of $1,500 had already been made out at the time of Sarazen's double eagle. Wood eventually recovered from the shock and disappointment of losing, as well as being the goat who was knocked out by Sarazen, and six years later redeemed himself by winning a Masters title of his own.

Gene Sarazen's career was noteworthy for several reasons, and he was inducted into the Golf Hall of Fame. He accomplished a career Grand Slam in majors, and sported his trademark plus-fours during his entire playing days, even while appearing as a commentator on TV. He lived a long, productive life until his death at age 97 in the year 1999, remembered and revered for his golfing knowledge and engaging personality that made him a sought-after ambassador of the game. But as rarely as a double eagle occurs, it is equally rare for the name of Gene Sarazen to be mentioned without referring to the moment that defined him, "the shot heard 'round the world."

The Concession

Jack Nicklaus, Tony Jacklin, Ryder Cup

The first of the international tournaments now known as the Ryder Cup was played in 1921 at Gleneagles, Scotland. The format was originally conceived by a fellow named James Harnett, a circulation agent for *Golf Illustrated* magazine who proposed the idea of competition between American and British teams, and eventually got the financial backing he needed from the PGA of America.

The "rivalry" envisioned by Harnett started off as more of a rout, however, with the Brits delivering a sound trumping by a score of 9 points to 3. And when they got together again in 1926 for an unofficial match, the defeat was even more humiliating, a trouncing of the Americans to the tune of 13½ to just 1½.

There was a bright side to that year's contest, though. It had been witnessed by an entrepreneurial English seed merchant by the name of Samuel Ryder, an avid amateur golfer who was tutored in the game by the British professional Abe Mitchell. When the matches were completed, Ryder was enjoying tea with a group that included both Mitchell and the American Walter Hagen, when someone suggested that Ryder consider donating a trophy that would encourage a formal continuation of the British-American competition. The idea appealed to Ryder, who commissioned a piece that included a likeness of Mitchell, his mentor. Thus began the event now known as the Ryder Cup.

There is a unique aspect to the Ryder Cup competition: no prize money. It is played out of a sense of pure competition, with the victorious team being given only the honor of playing for their country and keeping possession of the Cup until the next contest two years later. Nevertheless, appointment to the team is a coveted tribute and hotly sought after by the top players from both sides.

Given the nobility and dignity conceived with this tournament's origin, as well as the gentlemanly behavior expected of golfers, one would assume that the contestants would hold themselves to the highest standards of behavior, and for the most part that is how it goes. But there are exceptions, most notably the competition in the year 1969, when members of both teams broke the unwritten code with some rather nasty behavior.

The Ryder Cup now includes players from all of Europe in addition to the British, so the Americans take on the best from the entire continent. But in 1969 it was still the United States against England, and the Americans had piled up a string of victories starting a decade earlier, so it's likely that the British players were under considerable pressure to pull out a win for a change. Perhaps that's why the conduct on both sides degenerated so badly. For example, the Brits had been instructed by their captain not to look for any American ball that had been lost in the rough, and one of the Americans purposely stood far too close to a British player as he was attempting to putt. Eventually, each team's captain had to call his belligerent players together and calm them down before things got really out of hand.

Meanwhile, neither team had a significant advantage in the scoring, and the final result came down to the match between America's Jack Nicklaus and Britain's Tony Jacklin, both of whom had managed to behave as gentlemen during the fray. It all came down to the last hole and the last putt, a 2-foot knee knocker that fell onto the shoulders of Tony Jacklin. It was only a 2-footer, but surely Jacklin was a tad nervous because there was so much riding on the result. A miss would have given the Americans the victory, while sinking the putt would result in a draw. At that point Nicklaus did something that would change the tone of the entire tournament: He conceded the putt to Jacklin, eliminating any possibility of a humiliating miss and assuring the draw. The gesture became known as "The Concession," an example of class and dignity that would be admired and remembered throughout the world of golf, and not surprisingly led to a lifelong friendship between Nicklaus and Jacklin.

The Ryder Cup has since seen an instance or two of tension between the two sides, but for the most part, the example of "The Concession" continues to influence the atmosphere of camaraderie that was originally intended by Samuel Ryder when he donated his coveted cup so many years ago.

A Love Affair
Bobby Jones, St. Andrews

Not every great romance, as we know, is love at first sight. Sometimes, it takes a while before the attraction burns brightest. Such was the relationship between the legendary Bobby Jones and the town of St. Andrews in Scotland.

Jones's first encounter with the Old Course at St. Andrews took place at The British Open in 1921. It didn't exactly go well. During the third round, on the eleventh hole, Jones found one of the notoriously deep bunkers. After one, two, three, and a fourth mighty swipe, Jones's ball remained in that pit of hell. The infuriated American was so distraught that he picked up his ball and tore up his scorecard. Not surprisingly, Jones made his disdain for the Old Course quite clear, and the British press reciprocated in kind, stating, "Master Bobby is just a boy, and an ordinary boy at that."

There came a moment when a little spark burst into a flame of love. After winning The British Open in 1926 at Royal Lytham & St. Annes, Jones returned to the scene of the crime at the Old Course in 1927. This time, things went differently, and that little love spark came from Bobby's putter. Jones's stroke was in rare form that day as he sank putt after putt, and at the round's conclusion he hadn't missed a single one under 12 feet. And are you ready for this? On the fifth hole Jones lined up a putt from an estimated 120 feet out and like all of the others it fell dead into the cup. When the scorecard was tallied and signed, Jones's magical performance ended with a parsimonious twenty-eight putts for the round! Not surprisingly, his first-round score of 68 was the low round of the tournament. In fact it was one of only two rounds in which the field shot below 70. And here's a candidate for shocker of the century (sarcasm intended): Jones won the tournament by a dominating six strokes over Aubrey Boomer and Fred Robson.

And then, like taking your date out for a beautiful evening and following it up by sending flowers the next day, Jones made a gallant gesture. He declined to take his momentous trophy back home to Atlanta, insisting instead that it stay with his friends at the Royal and Ancient Golf Club.

By now the folks at St. Andrews had become dedicated Bobby Jones fans, and if they weren't completely enamored with him after his chivalrous behavior in 1927, Jones became the last amateur to win on the Old Course in 1930, a year during which he just happened to win the Grand Slam.

Twenty-eight years later, in 1958, Bobby Jones was only the second American ever honored as a Freeman of the City of St. Andrews, the first being Benjamin Franklin all the way back in 1759. And today, one of the most prestigious scholarships in the world, aptly named the Robert T. Jones Scholarship, is sponsored by the collaboration of three academic institutions: Emory University and the Georgia Institute of Technology in Atlanta, Georgia, and the University of St. Andrews in Scotland.

While the relationship between Bobby Jones and St. Andrews got off to a rocky (or *sandy*) start, even now, in the twenty-first century, four decades after his death, Bobby Jones is still remembered and revered in St. Andrews as one of their most beloved sports heroes.

Always Happy

Tsuneyuki "Tommy" Nakajima,
The Masters, Open Championship

If you've never heard of a place by the name of Gunma Prefecture, you're not alone. It is located in the northwest corner of the Kanto region on Japan's Honshu Island. "Oh, sure," you might say, rolling your eyes, "the Kanto region. I've always wanted to visit there."

So what's the deal with Gunma Prefecture? It's the homeland of a very talented golfer by the name of Tsuneyuki "Tommy" Nakajima, who was born there on October 20, 1954. Tommy was attracted to golf at a young age, and after investing countless hours on the links as a junior, he made the leap to the professional ranks in 1975.

Generally speaking, Nakajima's chosen vocation has served him well, as he made quite a mark in the sport. He currently ranks third on the list of Japan's most golf tour victories with forty-eight to date. In addition, he was the top Japanese tour money earner in 1982, 1983, 1985, and 1986, and was ranked in the top ten in the world for eighty-five weeks during the mid-1980s.

But Nakajima would make his big splash several years before his career really took off. Entering the 1978 Masters, he was still trying to establish himself as a top-notch golfer. And like all the professionals in this heralded event, Nakajima was surely hoping to play some of his best golf. But as he played the par five thirteenth hole, known as the "Azalea Hole," let's just say things didn't go according to plan. He started off well enough, but when his fourth shot found Rae's Creek, Tommy made the perilous decision to play his ball from the water rather than take a drop, thus setting off a cataclysm of unfortunate events. First he popped his ball straight up into the air and back down right on his foot, resulting in a two-shot penalty. Then, as the bewildered golfer attempted to hand his club to his caddie, it slipped out of his hand and landed in the creek, another two-stroke penalty. This was followed by a chip that went over the green. When it was finally, mercifully over, the man from Japan had managed to two-putt for a dispiriting tally of thirteen strokes, thus tying a record for high score on any single hole at The Masters. Needless to say, Nakajima's dream of winning the 1978 Masters was over before he reached the fourteenth tee.

His horrendous Masters experience was certainly more than enough for anyone to absorb, especially in one year. But the golf gods weren't finished playing tricks on poor Tommy. Even the vast expanse of the Atlantic Ocean wasn't enough for him to escape their mischievous torture. Later in that very same year, at the 1978 Open Championship at St. Andrews, Nakajima was in contention during the third round, actually tied for the lead as he approached hole number seventeen. And that's when déjà vu happened all over again. He stroked his putt, then watched it roll, and roll, completely off the green and into the Road Hole bunker. Once again things went from bad to worse when it took him not one, not two, not three, but four attempts to get out of the deep trap. Final result? A quintuple bogey nine. And to add insult to injury, this infamous bunker is now often referred to as "The Sands of Nakajima."

Despite a very respectable career, Tommy Nakajima never would win that elusive major title, his best ever finish being third at the 1988 PGA Championship. Ironically, Nakajima's given name of Tsuneyuki translates to "Always Happy," but he was probably wondering if that translation was all that meaningful during those two catastrophic golf holes in 1978.

Making History

Thomas Weiskopf, The Masters

There's just something about The Masters. The magnificent setting; springtime gloriously bursting forth with dogwood blossoms and reborn greenery; newly mown grass that you can practically smell through your television set; the signature music and mellifluous voices of the announcers. There's a dreamlike quality, a gentility that soothes one's soul while simultaneously awakening competitive juices, so that virtually every golfer—weekend hacker, club champion, or aspiring professional—has pictured themselves in Butler Cabin, being interviewed on worldwide television and donning that legendary green jacket as the Masters Champion.

Thomas Daniel Weiskopf was surely one of the many Masters dreamers. Born on November 9, 1942, in Massillon, Ohio, Tom picked up the game as a youngster, and after a strong junior career, he took his talents to Ohio State, where he was part of the Buckeye golf team. After turning professional in 1964, Weiskopf would win his first PGA title in 1968 at the Andy Williams-San Diego Open Invitational. In 1973 he won seven tournaments, including his first major at The British Open at Royal Troon. Still in his prime, Weiskopf had become the second ranked golfer in the world, and had the talent and the aspirations to reach number one!

With thoughts of immortality now racing through his head, Weiskopf was surely expecting to add more major titles to his trophy case. And where better to do so than at Augusta? Many pundits had noted that he had the perfect swing to succeed at The Masters, and he had already finished in second place on two separate occasions, in 1969 and 1972.

But history repeated itself when Weiskopf was a Masters's bridesmaid again in 1974 and 1975. As the years continued to pass and he repeatedly failed to win another major, Weiskopf must have felt that Father Time was working against him. So when he came to The Masters yet again in 1980, he felt the pull of history and was determined to leave his mark.

Playing in his first round, Weiskopf prepared to tee off at the dangerous 155-yard, par three twelfth hole. Because this sinister little stretch of greenery was known as one of the most treacherous in golf, Weiskopf knew he had to be careful. He drew a seven iron out of his bag and struck it cleanly, but regrettably with a bit too much backspin. The ball landed on the green but then spun back off the putting surface and down the steep bank and into Rae's Creek. Frustrated by this misfortune, Weiskopf proceeded to the drop area, where he hit his next shot into the drink as well. And then, annoyance evolving first into anger and then into a crisis of confidence, he found the water on his next three shots, too! In case you weren't counting, Weiskopf hit the water on *five* successive shots before finally landing his ball on the back fringe and mercifully two-putting. At last the nightmare was over, but by that time he had taken a total of thirteen shots, tying The Masters record for the highest score on a single hole . . . and this was on a par three!

Despite this calamity, Weiskopf's career was far from over. He continued to play his magnificent brand of golf, eventually achieving his sixteenth and final PGA Tour victory at the 1982 Western Open. As for The Masters, his lifelong quest to make history in Augusta was ultimately accomplished, but sadly not for winning the title. Instead, he has the dubious distinction of holding two unwanted records. First, for a player who has never won The Masters, Weiskopf has more second-place finishes than anyone else. And as we are all now aware, his 13 on the par three twelfth in 1980 ties him for the highest one-hole score in the history of the tournament.

Never Give Up

Mark Francis O'Meara, The Masters

"When the going gets tough, the tough get going!"
"Try, try again!"
"I think I can, I think I can!"
"Winners never quit, and quitters never win!"
"You can't win if you don't try!"
(Go ahead. I'll bet you can add a couple other platitudes to this list.)

It is said that the true sign of greatness is to never give up. When facing long odds, when your back is against the wall, when things look their bleakest . . . to pull yourself up by your bootstraps and forge ahead can often be the difference between success and failure, and sometimes result in greatness.

A case in point:

Mark Francis O'Meara was born on January 13, 1957, in Goldsboro, North Carolina. By today's standards Mark was a latecomer to golf, starting the game at the ancient age of thirteen, when he would sneak onto the Mission Viejo Country Club course in Southern California. After becoming an employee at that same Mission Viejo Club and joining his high school team, Mark began to show real promise. He then entered Long Beach State University, where he was named an All-American, and in 1979 he announced he was for real by claiming victory at the US Amateur. At this point he was ready to join the professional ranks and did so in 1980.

O'Meara's professional playing days took awhile to get off the ground, but as would be his M.O. throughout his whole career, he persevered. After grinding it out for four long years, he finally managed to take his first PGA event, winning the 1984 Greater Milwaukee Open by five strokes. Now that he had broken through, he would back up that victory with another thirteen PGA titles, for a total of fourteen by the time he had reached his fortieth birthday. Presumably his career would be downhill from then on, but it had been a successful run by almost anyone's standards, and more money than he had ever imagined as a youth.

There was still an empty space in his trophy collection. A championship at a major had eluded him. And he refused to accept the conventional wisdom that one's career was all but over when you have reached "a certain age." He kept his dream alive, and in 1998 he traveled to Augusta, Georgia . . .

As he entered The Masters that year, the name Mark O'Meara was nowhere to be found on the list of likely winners, and after a 74 in the first round, he was already five shots off the lead. He showed improvement in round two, shooting a solid 70, but again found himself five shots back. Still, that was more than good enough to make the cut, and when the weekend started, his game went into high gear. Saturday's score was even better, a 68. Now he was actually in the hunt!

On the final Sunday O'Meara stayed within striking distance, and that's when he showed his stuff. A pair of birdies late on the back nine tied him for the lead, and on hole number eighteen he found his opportunity, a 20-foot putt for birdie and the championship. Make it, and his lifetime dream would come true.

In a scene that was viewed by millions on countless replays, the ball found the bottom of the hole and our slightly portly hero soared through the air like a superhuman Baryshnikov. (Well, maybe not quite that balletic, but I'm pretty sure he at least jumped high enough to slide a credit card beneath his feet.) No matter, he may have remained earthbound, but he was The Masters Champion, and well deserved.

It had taken fifteen attempts, more than any other golfer who had ever won The Masters, but Mark O'Meara had taken to heart the inspirational sayings at the beginning of this story; he had never given up, and in the end he had left his mark on history, even after most pundits considered that his best days were behind him.

Oh, and I forgot to mention . . . just three months later, this same never-say-die guy hit it big again, winning his second major, the prestigious British Open.

So there you have it. "Never give up!" "Keep your eye on the prize." "Don't hang your head." "Pay no attention to the naysayers." "You can do it!"

And finally, the one you heard from your mother so many times: "*Somebody* has to win. Why shouldn't it be you?"

World's Longest Hole-in-One
Bill Morse, Farmington

Just a few miles west of the Connecticut state capital of Hartford lies the upscale suburb of Farmington, an idyllic, verdant little hamlet with tight zoning laws, tasteful homes, and the requisite wine and antiques shops. Near the center of town one can find the prestigious Farmington Country Club with its imposing, white-pillared clubhouse, a regal structure that smacks of grandeur and old money. One pictures elegant, white-haired couples clad in pink and green, sipping twilight cocktails under Chinese lanterns, the women discussing their volunteer charity work while their men pat each other's backs and clink glasses to celebrate successful business deals, all in good taste of course.

But there's more to this institution than stuffy formality. In fact, the rear of the building provides a different scene, one that's a lot less formal and at times even a bit raucous. They know how to play golf at the Farmington club, and they know how to enjoy themselves, too. The banter is friendly, the beer is cold—often drunk straight out of longneck bottles—and there's a general air of camaraderie that's truly inviting.

Now picture a Saturday morning in May 1997 where a number of folks are on the veranda, waiting their turn to tee off. Meanwhile they're taking in the expansive view, which includes the first tee and fairway on the right side of their vista, plus the fairway and green on hole number eighteen, well off to the left and down a gently slant-ing hill. When a golfer's shot is well executed, he's likely to hear polite applause, or maybe a call of "good shot," but a duck hook or banana slice is likely to inspire some good-natured groans or cat-calls, especially if the shot was made by someone who's well-known and well-liked.

Which brings us to that fateful Saturday morning in May and a gentleman by the name of Bill Morse, a good amateur golfer who was the former club champion. Bill happened to be celebrating his fifty-first birthday that day, and he ended up doing so in a way that was, well, *unusual*.

The first fairway at Farmington is a dogleg left, so while standing on the tee, one has a few choices: Play safe to the middle of the fair-way; try a draw to decrease the distance on the approach shot; or cut the corner by skimming to the right side of a stately spruce tree. Well, it seems that Morse took the shortest route that morning. He caught the ball cleanly off the tee, but then he, the others in his foursome, and the twenty or so observers on the veranda all held their breath as the ball came dangerously close to that big spruce.

Then there was an uh-oh. The ball caught the tree, and surely there was going to be an unplayable lie. But the ball didn't stop. It sailed through the branches, banged off some rocks near a cart path, and to the delight of all the observers, landed on the left front of *the eighteenth green,* continued rolling, and ended up plopping right into the cup!

According to Bill Morse, while the ball was rolling, "Everyone started yelling for the ball to go in. And when it did, I raised my arms in triumph, then fell down in laughter along with everyone else. The guy who had to tee off after me could barely keep it together."

Now there have been some pretty spectacular aces in the history of golf, even including a few on short par fours. And there have also been some outrageously long drives, including the one mentioned elsewhere in this collection that went well more than a mile on a long stretch of Antarctic ice. But I defy anyone, pro or amateur, to try matching this one, the longest hole-in-one in history, 6,411 yards!

Epilogue

The newspaper article about this wacky incident was proudly posted in the clubhouse, and was often the first thing shown to a new guest. And believe it or not, two years later the same Mr. Morse actually had a legitimate hole-in-one, also at Farmington Country Club, and also—you guessed it—on that same hole number eighteen, a 205-yard par three.

Always Follow the Rules
Paul Farmer, Texas Open

As easy as it appears, golf can be a devilishly difficult sport. The ball is just sitting there. It's not even moving. Surely it shouldn't be that difficult to hit it cleanly, and in the right direction, especially after years of lessons and practice. But alas, appearances can be deceiving. A new golfer typically assesses the challenge of the game, concludes that it can't be that difficult, then proceeds to encounter the rude awakening that we all had the first time we played. It's uncanny. The doggone game simply waits for its unsuspecting patsies, then sets forth a set of variables that could, and has, filled volumes. But who knows? Perhaps it's this paradoxical difficulty that keeps us coming back for more.

So I think we've established that golf is complicated enough and we need not make it any harder than it already is. But apparently the physical aspect of the game was not enough for the powers that be. On top of the aforementioned difficulties, they have added a thick book of rules that are often impossible to keep straight. You've seen it dozens of times on TV. A player comes upon an unusual lie and you think, "How difficult can it be to decide what to do?" Then the player and a tournament official stand there forever, mulling over a ruling on how, or where, the shot may be played.

Now I realize that every sport has a long list of rules, but generally we can all keep track of them, even if some may be a bit obscure. But how many times do we see the professionals, the folks making a living playing the game, screw up and receive a subsequent penalty? It truly baffles the mind. Who can forget the case of Craig Stadler, a man faced with having to hit a ball while on his knees, then who got penalized simply because he knelt on a towel to protect his pants from a damp spot? Or the heartbreaking "What a stupid I am!" incident when Roberto De Vicanezo innocently signed an errant scorecard, thus forfeiting a tie at the 1968 Masters and a chance to win in a playoff the following day?

This brings us to the 1960 Texas Open, where there was an incident so bizarre it boggles the mind. Paul Farmer may not be a household name, but like most professionals he was trying to eke out a living playing the game he loved. As Farmer competed at the Fort Sam Houston Golf Course in San Antonio, things were moving along smoothly. But when he finished his front nine, he noticed that the paint on his putter was peeling just a bit. Not to worry, thought Farmer. He simply replaced the club and continued with his round. And the new putter served him well, so much so that after finishing the eighteenth hole, he must have been pleased with his round of 70.

But hold on there, partner. When word of Farmer's putter switch got back to the officials, they quickly informed the shocked golfer that he had engaged in a violation of the exacting rules of golf. Because his putter was not judged to be "broken," it was illegal to switch it. The result? A staggering two-stroke penalty for each and every hole played with the tainted weapon. When all was said and done, Farmer incurred an astounding eighteen penalty strokes, ballooning his final score from a round of 70 to a gut-wrenching 88! Needless to say, the hapless Mr. Farmer did not win the tournament but did learn a valuable lesson. As every kindergarten teacher in the country will tell you, "Always follow the rules."

To Be Rich

Arnold Palmer, First Million-Dollar Career

Wouldn't it be amazing to be a professional golfer? For one, you would get to play golf for a living! And of course, "A bad day on the golf course beats a good day at work." Secondly, you would be the envy of all your family and friends. And if you were lucky enough to excel at your craft, you would be famous. Oh, and did I forget to mention that you just might be rich beyond your wildest dreams?!

Yet the monetary success of a Tiger Woods or a Phil Mickelson is a relatively new aspect to the professional game. For years, in order to play the Grand Slams, you needed to maintain your amateur status. And even as recently as a few decades ago, the idea of a million-dollar payday for a single golf victory seemed like something out of a fairy tale.

But thanks to the pioneers of the sport, today's best players can make tens, and even hundreds of millions of dollars over a career. In fact, today's superstars owe a great debt of gratitude to the golfers who laid the groundwork for today's financial abundance. And in my opinion, there is no golfer who deserves more recognition for this than the great Arnold Palmer.

When Palmer turned professional in 1954, the players on tour were fighting it out for a mere pittance compared to today's prize money. Back in the mid-twentieth century a golfer played as much for the love of the sport as he did for a mega mansion and a personal jet. Even so, Arnie still managed to earn a pretty good living. He claimed sixty-two PGA tour victories throughout his illustrious career, including an impressive seven victories in the majors. These numbers place him fifth on the PGA leader board. But in 1968, when he was thirty-eight years old, many golf pundits were speculating that Arnie's career might be over.

The trouble started when he missed the cut at the '68 Masters. He would follow that up with a lackluster performance at that year's US Open, where he placed fifty-ninth. And as he entered the 1968 Kemper Open, he was in the midst of an eight-month winless drought. But contrary to the pundits' opinion, Arnold believed that he still had more to give. And it should have come as no surprise that he found his game again, shooting an impressive 69, 70, and 70 over the first three rounds. Now that he was in contention, he wasn't about to let this one slip away. Coming back from three strokes down, he shot a final round of 67 to take the title, and in doing so became the first golfer to earn a total of $1 million over the course of his career.

Arnold Palmer would go on to win another eight PGA titles, his last coming at the Bob Hope Desert Classic on February 11, 1973. Obviously he has done quite well for himself, but this was due mainly to a variety of successful business ventures. True, it was his name and reputation that gave him entré into these investments, but by current financial standards his golfing victories produced only a fraction of what the top players make. Today's multimillionaires owe Mr. Palmer a very big debt of gratitude, because it was due in large part to his trailblazing career that the sport of golf now commands the kind of purses that were unimaginable just one generation ago.

Keep On Hackin'

John Ball Jr., British Amateur, British Open

Although the "modern" version of golf began in fifteenth-century Scotland almost five centuries ago, and other forms of the sport were played in other civilizations even before then, when most of us think about the game, we picture bucolic settings, beautifully maintained fairways and greens, elegant country clubs, and equipment that have evolved into powerful, accurate tools. In the right hands, these instruments are capable of pushing the limits of the game beyond anything golf's founders could have imagined. In comparison, the courses, layouts, clubs, and balls of yesteryear were almost laughably primitive. But even with such crude equipment, those old-timers were capable of playing some very impressive golf.

An excellent example is a gentleman by the name of John Ball Jr., one of the greatest golfers in Great Britain around the turn of the twentieth century. Born on December 24, 1861, in Hoylake, England, Ball would dominate golf in the British Isles on a level that was comparable to the legendary Bobby Jones's supremacy in the United States.

Showing early promise, the young Mr. Ball would first play The British Open in 1878, finishing fifth at the age of seventeen. And it took only one more year for him to claim the British Amateur title, defeating J. E. Findlay at Prestwick, 5 and 4 in the final.

He would win, eventually, an astounding total of eight British Amateur championships.

According to all accounts, Ball's swing was truly a thing of beauty. As stated by Bernard Darwin, "I have derived greater aesthetic and emotional pleasure from watching John Ball than from any other spectacle in the game." Apparently this opinion was held by quite a number of golfers, because others were known to wax even more enthusiastically in his praise. So classic was his swing and so transcendent was his game that the British golf historian Donald Steele would later state, "No golfer ever came to be more of a legend in his own lifetime." High praise indeed.

But Ball's best season was surely 1890. Not only did he win the British Amateur championship yet again, but he was also vying to win The British Open. This was not an easy task. As of the year 1890, no golfer had ever won the British Amateur championship and British Open in the same year. But John Ball was undeterred and determined to make history.

Playing at the Prestwick Golf Course in Scotland, Ball was at the top of his game when things suddenly got tricky. Prestwick featured an enormous bunker that was known as the Half Moon. When Ball's shot landed in this giant sand cavern, he evaluated the scene, approached the ball, and took a mighty swipe. But he was not able to extricate himself. Undeterred, he set his sights again and took another cut. The result? Still in the trap. Then another shot. No luck, still in prison. Then another, and another, and another, a total of *eleven* shots to get out of that sinister bunker, one that must have been designed by someone with a dark sense of humor.

Who could blame anyone for giving up after such a fiasco? But John Ball would have none of it. Eleven shots, and still not dispirited. In what can only be considered a true testament of will and determination, John kept his head down, forged ahead, and still won the tournament by three strokes! As history would prove, only Bobby Jones would repeat Ball's British double when he took the British Amateur and British Open in 1930.

John Ball Jr. is truly one of the game's legends. He died on December 2, 1940, but would be posthumously inducted into golf's Hall of Fame in 1977. And to further illustrate the extent of his impact on the sport, he was the first amateur golfer in England to be named an "immortal" by the Royal Empire. Heady stuff indeed, and clearly well deserved.

Whiff

Al Chandler, Senior Players Championship

There's a lot to love about the great game of golf. Booming a drive straight down the fairway, getting up and down from a treacherous trap, sinking a long putt, the glorious scenery, the camaraderie of playing with a few of your buddies, discussing the round over a cold one in the nineteenth hole, the list goes on and on. But as mentioned in the introduction to this book, at times we amateurs can obtain as much pleasure from watching the professionals perform as we do from teeing it up ourselves.

And most of us—while we feel sorry for a professional who makes a terrible blunder—also manage to derive a bit of sinister pleasure when he or she screws up. Just knowing that this glorious game can humble even the best there is makes us feel just a wee bit better when we slice a fifth consecutive drive into the woods. The Germans have a term for this: *schadenfreude*. Which means taking pleasure from the misfortune of others.

This brings me to the 1986 Senior Players Championship and a gentleman by the name of Al Chandler, who was one of the many professionals vying for the title. Clearly, Chandler was a talented individual, a man who had spent a lifetime practicing and preparing for just such an opportunity, and the chance at greatness was his for the taking.

As he played the fifteenth hole at the Canterbury Country Club located outside of Cleveland, Ohio, Chandler knew that every shot counted. But when his ball landed precariously close to an oak, he faced a sticky situation. The ideal would be to catch the ball cleanly and, of course, avoid contact with the tree. Should one take a full swing and catch the tree's solid base, or even a thick root, the result could be a serious injury such as a broken finger or wrist.

After discussing the options with his caddie, Chandler grabbed his weapon, addressed the ball, and took a calculated swat. The result: a big, fat whiff. The embarrassed golfer stepped back and took a moment to compose himself. He then approached the ball again, blocked out all distractions, took another swipe, and . . . another whiff! Now with the frustration of a caged lion, Chandler took one more cut and mercifully made contact and continued on with the hole. Ah . . . but this story is not yet over. When the nightmare hole was finally coming to a conclusion, and there was nothing left to do but to tap in his putt, the rattled golfer casually poked at the ball and incredibly missed everything again for his third whiff on the very same hole!

Golf is truly a great game. As the legion of weekend hackers can attest, there are few things more thrilling than playing a good round, and then posting a score that's a personal best. But when those bad days come, and nothing seems to be going well, I implore you to keep Al Chandler in mind. If even a seasoned professional can whiff three times on a single hole, surely you and I are entitled to a three-putt now and again.

Repeating History

Wayne Desmond Grady,
Phoenix Open, Los Angeles Open

We've all heard it a thousand times, the weighty statement of the famed Spanish philosopher George Santayana: "Those that don't learn from history are doomed to repeat it." This was clearly a lesson that the Australian golf professional Wayne Desmond Grady learned the hard way.

Grady was born on July 26, 1957, in Brisbane, Australia. After putting in hours and hours of work and dedication as an amateur, he made the leap to the professional ranks in 1978 and found immediate good fortune on the Australasia Tour when he won the Westlakes Classic that same year. A long dry spell followed, but he would find his game again in 1984. First he would win on the European Tour, claiming his second career professional tournament at the Lufthansa German Open, and that same year he would earn his PGA Tour card when he successfully navigated Qualifying School. These successes were followed by another winless streak of two years, so that by the time he entered the 1986 PGA season, Grady was surely wondering when the next victory would come his way.

With high hopes, Grady teed off at the Phoenix Open in January 1986. As he played his way into the tournament, his sole focus was on each and every shot. But when the Australian played a ball he believed was his own, an unforgivable no-no occurred. Wayne had actually struck another competitor's ball and was immediately disqualified. The disheartened golfer had no recourse but to leave the tournament with his tail between his legs.

The following month, Grady was ready to get back on track when he entered the Los Angeles Open. With the disaster in Phoenix behind him, he was dreaming about getting back into the winner's circle, but in an uncanny déjà vu experience, Grady played the wrong ball yet *again*, and was once more immediately disqualified. In an unprecedented set of events, Wayne Grady was not only disqualified twice for playing the wrong ball, but it happened in successive months!

Thankfully, this story has a happy ending. While some golfers might never recover from such disheartening events, Grady came back to win another seven professional events for a total of nine throughout his career. And today, Wayne Grady is remembered most not for his blunders in 1986 but for his historic major victory at the 1990 PGA Championship, which he won by three strokes.

Happily, Mr. Grady was more than able to shake off the ignominy of those two wrong-ball incidents, because his pursuits after retiring from the professional tour have been quite successful. Since 2005 he has been the chairman of the Australian PGA Tour board and owner of a golf tour company and a golf course design business. He is also noted for working from time to time for the BBC televised golf coverage. And there's one more thing.

Even if he isn't a history buff, Wayne has surely committed one very important golf principle to memory: "Keep your eye on the ball." (But just make sure it's *your* ball!)

Old-Timer

Julius Boros, US Open, PGA Championship

One of the many, many things I love about golf is that it's a lifetime sport. While some other activities, like football and baseball, limit your playing time to your youth, golf can be played at a high level well into your older years. Consider the golfers who shoot their age in their seventies, eighties, and even nineties. Truly, this is a sport you can play, and play well, until the day you die.

Julius Nicholas Boros was born on March 3, 1920, in Bridgeport, Connecticut. Early on, Boros made a living as an accountant and didn't become a professional golfer until 1949, when he was already twenty-nine years of age. But he certainly didn't allow his late start to hold him back. Three years after his professional debut, he had his coming-out party when he won his first PGA tournament. And he did it in grand style, at nothing less than the 1952 US Open, by a commanding four strokes over runner-up Ed Oliver. Although he would win ten more tournaments over the next decade, another major title eluded him during that stretch. And then, eleven years after winning his first US Open, he won it again in 1963 at the age of forty-three in a playoff over Jacky Cupit and a player you may have heard of by the name of Arnold Palmer.

But now that Boros was well into his forties it appeared that his best days were behind him. Able to secure the Greater Greensboro Open title in 1964, and three more PGA titles in 1967, Boros's thoughts of winning a major title in his late forties seemed nearly impossible. Then again, while Mr. Boros may have been older than most of his competitors in terms of age, his laid-back style and love for the game kept him playing like a bright-eyed youngster.

And in 1968, just to prove that age is only a number, a forty-eight-year-old Boros shot a final round 69 for a four-day 281 total, defeating Bob Charles and (again) Arnold Palmer to win the PGA Championship. With this historic victory, Boros became the oldest player to ever win a major championship!

Boros's last PGA Tour victory would come less than a month later when he won the Westchester Classic, giving him a career total of eighteen PGA titles. In addition to this impressive collection, he was a member of the Ryder Cup in 1959, 1963, 1965, and 1967, and he also amassed more than $1 million in career earnings. He was inducted into the Golf Hall of Fame in 1982.

Julius Boros died of a fatal heart attack in 1994 while playing golf at the Coral Ridge Country Club in Fort Lauderdale, Florida. At the time he was found sitting in his golf cart under a willow tree near the sixteenth hole. It was said to be his favorite spot on the course.

Winner, Winner, Chicken Dinner
Dorothy Iona Campbell, Golf's Most Prolific Champion

"Show me a good loser and I'll show you a loser."
"If it doesn't matter if you win or lose, why do they keep score?"

While it is true that in sports we appreciate a player who gives it their all (even if they lose), and everyone loves an underdog, there isn't anything that the masses appreciate more than a winner. From Muhammad Ali to Mickey Mantle to Chris Evert to Wayne Gretzky, show me a champion and I'll show you a revered athlete. And of course golf is no exception. The most popular players throughout history have been the greatest winners. From Bobby Jones to Byron Nelson to Arnold Palmer to Jack Nicklaus to Tiger Woods . . . we just all love a champion.

But if one were to make a list of the most prolific winners of all time, that list would be woefully incomplete if it didn't include the name of Dorothy Iona Campbell.

Who?

Well, if I told you that her record would blow away her nearest rival, woman or man, would that pique your interest?

Dorothy Campbell was born on March 24, 1883, in North Berwick, Scotland, into a family that can only be described as golf fanatics. You've heard of being born with a silver spoon in your mouth. Well, how about being born with a putter in your hand? Believe it or not, Dorothy was swinging a golf club at the age of eighteen months, and just a few years later she was already competing against her older sisters. With a pedigree like that, there was little doubt that Campbell would make golf her life's mission. And oh, what a journey it would be!

Over the course of her heralded career, our heroine would be known by a variety of names, including Dorothy Hurd, Mrs. J. V. Hurd, Dorothy Howe, and the grandiose sounding Dorothy Campbell Hurd Howe. But whatever her name, she would win an astonishing eleven national amateur championships. Also among her many accolades: the first woman to win the British, US, and Canadian Women's Amateur titles.

And this lady was no flash in the pan. Dorothy just seemed to get better with age, continuing to rack up victory after victory. Despite moving to Canada in 1910, and three years later moving to the United States, she just kept on accumulating titles in droves. By the time her career had come to an end, Dorothy had won a staggering 750 (yes, *750*) tournaments!

Sadly, the first truly dominant female golfer of international notoriety would meet her death on March 20, 1945, when she was hit by a train. Even at that advanced age, who knows what more she might have accomplished? Yet Campbell's legacy cannot be denied. In a sports world where certain numbers carry the weight of gold (e.g., Joe DiMaggio's fifty-six-game hitting streak, the 17–0 undefeated 1972 Miami Dolphins, Jack Nicklaus's eighteen major championships), can any number truly compare to Dorothy Campbell's 750 tournament titles? Now that's a big number, and it's a very safe bet that her record will never be broken!

The Low Round

Homero Blancas,

Premier Invitational

Every golfer will admit it. They dream of that magical day when everything just clicks; the round where all the tee shots are ripped right down the middle of the fairway, all the iron hits are straight and true, and every putt finds the bottom of the cup. Wouldn't it be great to break 80? Or perhaps your goal is to shoot par. Or if you're willing to make a deal with the devil, how about a round in the 60s? Go ahead! Dare to dream!

As technology continues to evolve, golf clubs are now made from materials that seem to have come straight from the space program, and they're launching shots that make the golf ball appear to have afterburners. Combined with bigger and stronger athletes, scores have fallen lower and lower over the years. In fact, in today's professional game one doesn't even blink at rounds well below par, whereas not very long ago the same scores would have made front-page news.

But despite the vastly improved equipment and fitter athletes, there has continued to be an almost unapproachable bottom when it comes to scoring. A round in the 60s is one thing, and certainly no easy feat to pull off, but the magical number of 59 remains as the ultimate goal of even the pros. In fact, it has only happened three times on the PGA Tour. Al Geiberger was the first to pull it off when he shot a 59 during the second round of the Danny Thomas Memphis Classic in 1977; David Duval followed suit with a 59 of his own in the final round of the 1999 Bob Hope tournament; and most recently, Phil Mickelson's scorecard boasted a 59 after a stunning final round at the 2004 Grand Slam of Golf. As for the LPGA tour, this most impressive of achievements has been accomplished just once, by Annika Sorenstam when she shot a 59 during the second round of the Standard Register Ping tournament in 2001.

These rounds were truly incredible, and no doubt will be remembered for years to come. But if you think a 59 is so impressive that it could never be bested . . . well, just keep reading, because what's to come just might knock your socks off!

All the way back in 1962, the future PGA professional Homero Blancas was playing as an amateur at the Premier Invitational. Blancas must have thought he was dreaming that day, because every swing was pure, every club made perfect contact with the ball, every putt was true. After the front nine he had shot a ridiculously low score of 27.

Surely he knew that he couldn't keep up this pace on the back nine. And he was right. He didn't shoot another 27. He shot a 28. He had made a total of thirteen birdies and one eagle, and needed only twenty putts for the entire round.

Now for the math. As he sat in the clubhouse after the round, Homero must have needed to rub his eyes and check his score card twice, for he had shot an astonishing, improbable *fifteen-under-par 55*, the lowest score ever recorded in the history of tournament golf! And remember, he did this in 1962, with all of the equipment restrictions of the era.

Fifty years later no golfer has equaled the feat, so challengers beware. If you think you can match Homero's fantastic performance, or even beat it, go ahead and give it a try. Who knows? With a generous helping of luck, anything can happen. But before you announce your intentions to the regulars in your weekend foursome, let me offer just a wee bit of advice: *Leave your wallet at home!*

Million-Dollar Shot

Sheldon George "Don" Pooley Jr., Bay Hill Classic

No matter how badly one plays, or how frustrating the round, or as many times as a golfer swears he'll never pick up another club for as long as he lives . . . inevitably he comes back for more. But why? Why is it that after a lifetime of practice the wheels can just fall off and leave an otherwise psychologically healthy individual talking to himself like a mental patient? And yet inexplicably, like the lovestruck boy who allows the beautiful girl to repeatedly treat him like dirt, only to bring her flowers again the next day, we keep getting drawn back by golf. The answer? It's because we keep thinking the next time will be different:

"Next time I'll keep my left arm straighter."

"Next time I'll keep my head down."

"Next time I'll truly focus and that will make all of the difference."

And why do seemingly bright individuals fall for this apparent con time and time again? Because inevitably, no matter how bad a round we have, those tantalizing, tormenting golf gods let us hit at least one good shot—one moment of glory in the ocean of ineptitude. And if you're looking for a perfect example, consider the following:

Sheldon George "Don" Pooley Jr. was born on August 27, 1951, in Phoenix, Arizona, but grew up in Riverside, California. Pooley displayed a proficiency for the great game of golf, eventually taking his skills to the University of Arizona as part of the Wildcat golf team.

After a successful stint in Tucson, Pooley ascended to the next level, turning pro in 1973. On the tour, however, he faced the harsh reality of grinding it out for a long seven years. Eventually he would find the winner's circle by shooting four sub-70 rounds to win The B.C. Open in 1980, giving him a one-shot victory over Peter Jacobson. Another drought followed, even though he won the Vardon Trophy in 1985 for the lowest scoring average of the year. By the time Pooley entered the 1987 season, he was desperate for another win, and of course the big check that would come along with it.

Which brings us to the 1987 Bay Hill Classic, with $1 million on the line. Not for the winner's purse, though. This mega prize was offered on a promotional hole for a hole-in-one. Surely the money would be wonderful, but come on . . . the odds of a hole-in-one are what, like 100,000 to 1? And to ace a hole with a million-dollar kicker on the end of it . . . nearly impossible! Anyway, what the heck. You can't win if you don't play.

So Pooley adjusted for the wind, lined up his shot, and let it rip. And as you may have guessed . . . kerplunk, a million-dollar ace!

Pooley didn't receive a million, however. In actuality he got $500,000, with the other half million going to the Arnold Palmer Hospital for Children and Women in Orlando, Florida. Nevertheless, his one perfect stroke and the resulting ace resulted in a larger payday than he ever received for a whole year's worth of earnings.

Don Pooley would also win his second and last PGA title during the 1987 season when he was victorious at the Memorial Tournament. Then, following a series of ailments that put his career on hold for several years, he came back strong to win the US Senior Open in 2002. But despite his two PGA titles, the Vardon Trophy, and that incredible major senior's victory, Don Pooley is still remembered most for that sensational ace, a hole-in-one worth a cool million bucks!

221

It Ain't Over Till It's Over

John Flannery, Ben Hogan Reno Open

"It ain't over till it's over." We've all heard this expression a thousand times, and it's usually applied to sporting events. It happens time and time again: the contest seems to be over, completely out of reach; the fat lady is singing . . . and then, miraculously, fortune turns and the other guy (or team) snatches victory from the jaws of defeat.

A personification of this principle was one John Flannery, who was born in Salinas, California, on April 11, 1962. A California boy through and through, John would eventually take his golf game to USC, where he excelled on the Trojan golf team. Then, in 1985, he indulged his dream by turning pro. After two years he scored a victory at the 1987 California State Open, and now that he was a "winner" he had thoughts of bigger and better things. Still, he wasn't quite ready for the big time of the PGA Tour. He would have to fight it out in the trenches; i.e., the minor leagues of the Nationwide Tour.

As Flannery entered the 1991 Ben Hogan Reno Open, he was still looking for his first victory in a Nationwide event. But this time things were just different. Everything was clicking, and when he approached the eighteenth hole, he was in position to take home the title. In fact he had a par putt that just might win him the tournament. But his competitor, Esteban Toledo, was tied with Flannery and he also had a par putt, albeit slightly longer.

As Flannery went to mark his ball, he moved his marker a putter-head length away so as to stay out of Esteban's line. Toledo stroked his putt, but it missed its intended destination, giving Flannery a golden opportunity. John then lined up his ball, held his breath, and deftly putted it into the hole for his first Nationwide victory! The ecstatic golfer went to hug his caddie and shake hands with everyone on the green. And that's when the unthinkable happened: Flannery was informed that he replaced his ball in the wrong spot and would be penalized two strokes! And to make matters more complicated, after Flannery sank his putt, Toledo thought the tournament was over, so he directed his caddie to pick up his ball marker. That resulted in a one-stroke penalty to Toledo for not finishing the hole, so both players ended up with a double bogey. After all of that, the hole was halved, and the two dazed participants would be forced to enter a playoff.

So how did it turn out? Well, I guess you could say that justice prevailed, because Flannery won the hole with a par on the first playoff hole.

After his victory Flannery would gain some momentum by finishing the 1992 season with an additional three Nationwide titles. For his efforts, he was that year's leading tour money winner and would be named the 1992 Nationwide Player of the Year. His dream of playing on the PGA Tour would come true one year later, but after a lackluster performance he would eventually retire from professional golf in 2001.

It is said that one can earn quite an education out on the links, and it's probably safe to say that Mr. Flannery would agree that he learned a lifelong lesson from the 1991 Ben Hogan Reno Open: "It ain't over till it's over!"

Play On

Mike Reasor, Tallahassee Open

Athletes are notorious for staying on the field of play while injured. We've all heard the coach yell, "Suck it up! It's not that bad. Rub some dirt on it and get back in the game." But we can't blame it entirely on a callous coaching attitude. Often a player downplays the extent of his injuries in order to remain in the game, and this is bolstered by fans who admire their grit. In almost every sport, be it football, basketball, baseball, hockey, boxing, and even the gentlemanly sport of tennis, competitors frequently insist on continuing, even while they're at death's door, so long as there's still a chance to win. But what if I told you that golf is no exception? Now hold on. I know you're thinking, "Oh, c'mon. Golf's a great sport and all, but it's not exactly a bloodbath." Well, let me just give you one example to see if I can change your mind.

Mike Reasor was a lifelong resident of Seattle, Washington, who played on the PGA Tour from 1969 through 1978. And while Reasor is clearly not a household name, he did manage ten top-ten finishes during his days on the tour, and his failure to perform at a higher level certainly wasn't due to a lack of effort on his part.

In the middle of his PGA career, Reasor was playing in the 1974 Tallahassee Open, and he was doing well. So well in fact that he had made the cut after two rounds, and to celebrate his success he decided to relax by taking a horseback ride. Bad idea. Reasor

224

was thrown from the horse. The result was a separated left shoulder, damaged knee ligaments, and torn rib cartilage. Clearly there was no way that the ailing golfer could tee off again the next morning. But Reasor was a gamer who knew that every golfer who completed all four rounds of the Tallahassee Open would also be eligible for the following week's tournament. So what did the wounded warrior do? He decided to play one-handed! Reasor took out a five iron and played the third round with his right arm only, managing to finish with an impressive—under the circumstances—123. And in round four he started to get the hang of one-handed golf, improving enough to finish with a 114.

The good news was that his heroic effort made him eligible for the following week's event. But his final thirty-six-hole total of 237 is believed to be the highest ever two-round performance on the PGA Tour. And Reasor is also remembered for another dubious distinction. He happened to be Arnold Palmer's caddie at the 1966 US Open when Arnie fell apart on the final nine holes of the tournament and blew a seven-shot lead, eventually losing in a playoff to Billy Casper.

Despite his mixed legacy, Mike Reasor was clearly dedicated to the game of golf and would literally play until the day he died. While competing at the Pacific Northwest Section PGA Senior Championship in Bend, Oregon, Reasor was stricken with an apparent heart attack and died later that day. But one has to believe that if he could talk about his fate, Mike Reasor would maintain that he lived and died on his own terms. And while he surely left this world far too young, many a golfer would take Mike's deal, considering themselves fortunate if they could spend their last moments on earth on an idyllic, verdant golf course, sharing camaraderie with their playing partners, playing the game they love.

First Love

Maureen Riley, Western Pennsylvania

District Golf Championship

For those of us who truly love golf, it's almost constantly on our minds. Of course, nothing really beats being out on the course, playing a glorious round with a few of your closest friends, exulting over the good shots and commiserating over the calamities. But when that's not possible, when work and other impediments get in the way, the game is always with us and it seems like forever before we can get to our next round. For some people, though, the interval between rounds is a bit longer than others.

Maureen Riley was born on February 11, 1933, in the Pittsburgh suburb of Sharpsburg, Pennsylvania. Sharpsburg was a working-class town where many families were supported by men who earned their pay at the local steel mills, and of course women weren't even considered for such backbreaking work. The respective roles of men and women were quite clear. And of course there was also a sharp distinction between the activities considered appropriate for boys and girls. So Maureen's proud parents, Thomas and Zetta Riley, must have been quite progressive for the time as they permitted their daughter to join the boy's golf team at McKeesport High School in the 1940s. Surely there was some tongue wagging about the notion of a girl joining a boy's team, but the Rileys were undeterred. And as Maureen continued to play, her abilities and love for the sport blossomed, progressing to the point that she would later earn a ranking of the thirteenth best women's amateur in the United States.

Throughout her youth, Riley won title after title. One such victory was at the 1956 Western Pennsylvania District Golf Championship. Soon thereafter, however, she decided to give up the game she loved to marry and raise a family. The talented Miss Riley became Maureen Paladino, children soon followed, and golf was set aside, probably for good.

As one year turned into the next, and Mrs. Paladino was busy with day-to-day life, her golf tournaments were a distant memory. But the love of the game never left her. Many years later, when her kids were grown and had children of their own, something incredible happened. Maureen found herself back at the Western Pennsylvania District Golf Championship. It was 1998, forty-two years after the 1956 Championship. Incredibly, Maureen was victorious yet again. But the magnitude of the victory is not readily apparent until one looks inside the numbers.

So let's review those astonishing figures once more. As previously mentioned, Maureen first won the event in 1956 at the age of twenty-three, then as a grandmother at age sixty-five she won it again . . . after being away from playing the game competitively for forty-two years! And to throw in another crazy statistic, Maureen was six years older than the combined age of her three nearest competitors . . . truly amazing!

Over her golfing career, Maureen Riley Paladino was also a two-time Pennsylvania State Senior Women's Golf Champion, a two-time Pennsylvania State Super Senior Golf Champion, and an impressive eleven-time Sable Trace Women's Golf Champion. But it was Paladino's incredible second victory at the Western Pennsylvania District Golf Championship, forty-two years after her initial victory at the same tournament, for which she is most remembered. After the victory, Maureen was quoted as saying, "It was all I could do to keep my mind together. I'm no young chicken, you know."

Maureen would pass away on January 25, 2011, just shy of her seventy-eighth birthday. But her legacy will live on, and if we golfers have learned one thing from her amazing saga, it's that no matter what life throws at you, and no matter how long you are separated from the game, a true golfer will always come back to his or her first love.

For the Love of the Game
Chick Evans Jr.

As mentioned in the introduction of this book, your humble author loves golf. I love everything about it. From blasting a drive to a knee-knocking putt, I truly love the sport. So at times it can be disheartening when you see a professional who is simply going through the motions and appears to be disinterested, if not downright sick of the game. It's especially upsetting as most of us would give our right arm for a chance at life on the tour. But conversely, when a professional has all the money, fame, and titles one could ask for, and is still playing the game with a joyful exuberance, it warms one's cynical heart. And if we are looking for an example of a golfer who gave his life to the sport and kept coming back for more, not for money but for the sheer love of the game, we need look no further than Chick Evans Jr.

Charles E. Evans Jr. was born on July 18, 1890, in Indianapolis, Indiana, and would grow up on the north side of Chicago. Chick, as he was affectionately referred to, got his first taste of golf at the tender age of eight when he was given a job as a caddie at the Edgewater Golf Club near his home. It would be this part-time position that would set one of the greatest turn-of-the-twentieth-century golf careers into motion.

Evans was a quick study, worked hard, and dedicated his life to the game. In 1910, while playing as an amateur, Chick won the Western Open. (Incidentally, the only other amateur to date to win the Western Open was Scott Verplank in 1985.) But today, Chick is widely remembered for winning both the US Amateur and The US Open in the same year, when he pulled off the amazing double in 1916. This titanic feat has been duplicated by only one man, the legendary Bobby Jones.

But Evans's most impressive record isn't due to one specific tournament victory or one outstanding year. Instead, it is his consistent desire to play the game and his unwavering love for the sport. Case in point: Chick Evans played the US Amateur (a tournament with no prize money) for fifty ... yes, *fifty* consecutive years! And although he won it twice (1916 and 1920) and was a three-time runner-up, the fact that this man from humble beginnings would compete in this amateur competition for an incredible fifty straight years is, for me, an example of the finest behavior in our beloved sport.

In 1960 Evans was presented with the Bobby Jones Award, the highest honor a golfer can receive from the United States Golf Association in recognition of his distinguished sportsmanship. And it was entirely appropriate that he was inducted into the Golf Hall of Fame in 1975.

Chick Evans died on November 6, 1979, at the age of eighty-nine. He was a man who will be remembered for many accomplishments over the course of his career. But today, in this book, we remember him fondly for his pure love of golf.

Albatross

Sherri Turner, Atlanta Women's Championship

Chances are that you've heard the ultimate expression of ecstasy after a beautifully executed golf shot (or even blurted it yourself), "Damn! Better than sex!" Or how about, "Is there anything better than taking a long walk with just your putter in your hand?"

Really, what can compare with hitting that perfect shot? How great is it to watch your long drive go right down the middle of the fairway; your beautifully struck iron land only feet from the pin; your magnificently stroked putt creep up to the hole like a little mouse, and then dive into its lair.

But what about the ultimate in golf perfection? What about an ace . . . a hole-in-one? Now surely that's got to be the highest of highs on a golf course. But I'll do you one better. The rarest of golf feats . . . the albatross! A double eagle. Although it's been known to happen with a hole-in-one on a short par four, this once-in-a-lifetime shot (if that) normally occurs on a par five with a long drive off the tee, a second shot of pure brilliance, and a truckload of luck!

Sherri Turner was born in Greenville, South Carolina, on October 4, 1956, and was already playing golf by the age of five. During a brilliant amateur career, she would go on to win the 1974 and 1975 Carolina Junior Championship, and then take her talents to Furman University, where she earned All-American status in 1979.

Several years later, in 1984, Turner entered the LPGA with hopes for greatness. After so many years of paying her dues, she finally had her breakout year in 1988 when she won the LPGA Corning Classic and her first and only major at the LPGA Championship. And 1988 ultimately turned out to be a dream come true, as she was the top money winner and was later named the Golf Writers Association of America Female Player of the Year. The following year, in 1989, Turner won her third, and what would prove to be her final, LPGA title when she was victorious at the Orix Hawaiian Ladies Open, finishing the season a very respectable tenth on the money list. Staying near the top proved a bit too challenging, however. She managed to finish among the top forty money winners just two more times before retiring from the LPGA Tour in 2008. Still, her career was an overall success, and even those less productive years had their moments. Actually two moments in particular. Read on ...

In 1993, while playing the second round of the Atlanta Women's Championship at the Eagle's Landing Country Club in Stockbridge, Georgia, Turner approached the par five eighteenth hole and ripped a beautiful drive off the tee. The long shot left her with a rare chance to go for the green in two, and she went for it with gusto. She gripped it and ripped it, and watched in awe as her ball tracked beautifully toward the green. Along with the exuberant crowd, Turner watched as it rolled toward the hole, and then found the cup for a double eagle albatross! Now you may be thinking, "Okay, that's a great shot to be sure, but is this incident truly worthy of inclusion in a book of the most memorable moments in golf's long and illustrious history?" Again, read on!

Five years later, in 1998, while playing in the same tournament (now called the Chick-fil-A Charity Championship), Turner approached that same par five eighteenth hole, this time in the first round. And wouldn't you know it, history repeated itself! After another booming drive, the woman from South Carolina went for it once again, and in a perfect déjà vu moment the ball shot toward the green, was drawn to the hole as if by a magnet, and kerplunk! Another double eagle!

So how rare was this occurrence? Actually, Sherri Turner is believed to be the only individual to double eagle the same hole twice in competition on a US Tour.

Today Turner battles it out on the Legends Tour and even has one current victory to her credit (2008 BJ's Charity Classic). And while golf historians duly note her major LPGA victory in 1988, one still has to marvel over those two double eagles on the same hole, and under the pressure of professional competition. The odds have to be astronomical. But that's golf . . . just when you think you've seen everything . . . *shazam*! What a game!

Piggyback

Andrew Philip Parkin, British Open

Like most young golfers growing up in the United States, your humble author fantasized about one day winning the US Open. Sure, any of the major championships would be incredible, but to win our country's national championship . . . well, what could be better? And one can only assume that across the pond in Great Britain the lads have their own dreams of winning The British Open. And presumably, Andrew Philip Parkin was no exception.

Philip, as he was widely known, was born on December 12, 1961, in Doncaster, England, and grew up in Newtown, Powys. After a stellar junior career, Parkin made a rather vast leap, geographically and culturally, to play golf for the Texas A&M Aggies. He did well in his new environment, becoming the first Aggie, and first European, to earn first team All-American status. Soon afterward, he added the prestigious British Youth Championship to his resume, and the following year would win The Amateur Championship to become the only player to hold both titles at the same time. Then, after competing for the last time as an amateur at the 1984 Masters, Parkin took another giant step and turned pro.

Things started off well for Parkin, so well that he was named the 1984 Sir Henry Cotton Rookie of the Year on the European Tour. But he had his eye on even loftier goals, and as he entered the 1985 Open Championship, there was nothing he wanted more than to capture the Claret Jug. History was not on his side, however, because going into the 1985 British Open at Royal St. George's Golf Club in Sandwich, Kent, England, it had been sixteen long years since any Briton had won the event. Yet Parkin was undeterred and played some of his best golf in the first round to shoot a three-under-par 68. Now tied for second place, he was right in the mix. His score for the second round was a disappointing 76, however, and although he easily made the cut, he was well off the lead.

In the third round, things went from bad to worse when Parkin injured a muscle in his lower leg. The gutsy competitor was able to finish the round with a 77 but was now out of contention. Nevertheless, this was Parkin's national championship, and there was no way he wasn't going to give it his best effort on the final Sunday. Although hobbled by his injured leg, he took some pain-killing medication and came out for his final round. As the round wore on, the pills started to wear off and his pain became nearly unbearable. Parkin was later quoted as saying, "After ten it took me four minutes to move 100 yards and the pain almost made me cry. My dad came up and said, 'You can't go on,' and I said, 'You watch me.'"

Parkin popped some aspirin and gallantly played on. But at the seventy-second hole he could go no farther. At that point something incredible occurred. Parkin's playing partner, Nick Faldo, in a true display of sportsmanship and camaraderie, came to the wounded golfer's aid and literally threw the gimpy Brit on his back and carried him piggyback for the final 75 yards to the green. Incredibly, Parkin finished out the round with another 68 to equal his low round of the tournament. And although he played much of the tournament on only one good leg, Parkin finished tied for a respectable twenty-fifth place.

As to the tournament champion, there was no need to cry for Great Britain as the Scot, Sandy Lyle, ended his empire's winless streak by taking home the title. And in case you were wondering how the altruistic Englishman, Nick Faldo, fared, he finished in a disappointing tie for fifty-third. But no need to shed a tear for Nick either, as he would go on to win The British Open an incredible three times; 1987, 1990, and 1992. (Don't you just love karma?!)

War on the Shore

Hale Irwin, Bernhard Langer, Ryder Cup

Because golf is typically a solo sport with no one to rely on but one-self, pressure is an integral part of the experience. Surely we have all stood over a 3-foot knee-knocker putt with maybe $2 at stake, and gotten a case of the yips. So imagine what it's like to be part of a major championship, playing on the seventy-second hole with a putt to win a tournament that you have dreamed about since birth. Sound like pressure? Well, multiply it times a hundred and you have the Ryder Cup! It's one thing to play for yourself, but when you have your nation's fortunes riding on every shot, the tension of the moment can be monumental.

For a number of years, the Ryder Cup had been dominated by the Americans. However, in 1985 things took a turn as the Europeans reclaimed the cup with an outright victory.

The loss was something of a shock to the United States. It was the first time the American team had not prevailed since 1957. The Europeans won again in 1987, then retained the trophy two years later with only the second draw in the history of the competition. So needless to say, at the next meeting the Americans were desperate for a victory, and even more so because they were playing at home.

The 1991 Ryder Cup was played at Kiawah Island, South Caro-lina, on the majestic Ocean Course at the Kiawah Island Golf Resort. After the first day of competition the Americans held a slight 4½ to

3½ point advantage. But by the end of day two the Europeans had made up the deficit, and when the combatants arrived for the final day, the score was locked up at 8 points apiece.

As the Sunday singles matches unfolded, the tension was palpable. With so much riding on every shot, the players, the coaches, and the millions of spectators watching from around the globe knew that the fate of the cup could change at any single moment. But sure enough, as if the players weren't under enough pressure already, the rivalry came down to the final shot. The Americans were up 14 to 13 as Hale Irwin and Bernhard Langer battled on the final green. With their individual match tied, Langer needed to win the eighteenth hole to secure the match and force a Ryder Cup draw.

So the scene was set. Make the putt to force a draw and keep the cup, or miss and surrender it to the Americans. As Langer lined up his 6-footer, the moment was mesmerizing and yet excruciating. Finally, he made the stroke, and when his ball slid just right of the hole it was over. In a memorable picture, the euphoric Americans burst into celebration while the distraught German was being consoled by his teammates.

The 1991 Ryder Cup would come to be known as the "War on the Shore" and is now remembered as one of the most exhilarating, heart-wrenching, incredible golfing events in the history of the sport.

Phenom

Tiger Woods, The Masters

The legend of Tiger Woods began earlier in life than that of any other golfer in history. It actually started when he appeared as a two-year-old on the *Mike Douglas Show* in 1978 and demonstrated his putting prowess against comedian Bob Hope, leaving not only the hosts but also the television viewers in awe at what they had just witnessed. And that was just for starters. At age three he shot a 48 over nine holes at the Cypress Navy Course. But wait, there's more: At age five Tiger appeared on the ABC television show *That's Incredible* and at the same age was featured in *Golf Digest* magazine.

Flash forward a few years and Tiger again came into national prominence when he began competition as an amateur. As we are all now surely aware, Tiger Woods had one of the most storied amateur careers in the history of the sport. The shining moment came when he became the first golfer to win three consecutive US amateur titles, accomplishing this impressive feat in 1996 at age twenty.

Woods turned professional in August of 1996 and immediately signed lucrative endorsement contracts with Nike and Titleist. And when *Sports Illustrated* named him Sportsman of the Year, and he was also recognized as the PGA Rookie of the Year, the expectations went through the roof.

There were doubters, however. Pundits warned that even the most heralded of prodigies have disappeared from the limelight even quicker than they appeared. So when the 1997 golfing season began, all eyes were on one Eldrick Tont "Tiger" Woods. Would Tiger be a legend or a bust? Well, the world wouldn't have to wait long to find out.

As Tiger played the year's first major at The Masters in Augusta, Georgia, the pressure was enormous, enough so that he shot a disappointing 40 on the front nine. Again the pundits held forth. He was wilting under the heat of such an intense spotlight. But Tiger simply shook it off and recovered in sensational fashion, shooting an incredible 30 on the back nine for a first day total of 70. He then carried his momentum through day two with a sizzling 66 to take the tournament lead.

In round three, Woods was paired with the closest challenger, Colin Montgomerie. When Tiger shot a 65 as compared to Monty's 74, it was all but over. So much so that when Montgomerie was asked if it was possible for anyone to catch Woods, who now held a nine-shot lead over the field, Colin replied with a simple, "No chance." And on the final Sunday, wearing his trademark red shirt and black pants, Tiger closed with a 69. After sinking the final putt, Tiger pumped his fist and in a moment that could have melted a grinch's heart, he tearfully embraced his father who had mentored him.

History was rewritten that day. Tiger Woods became the youngest ever Masters Champion at the age of twenty-one; he posted the lowest ever seventy-two-hole score at The Masters with a 270; and he established the largest ever margin of victory at The Masters with a twelve-stroke advantage over runner-up Tom Kite.

Had there ever really been any doubt? If so, it popped like a delicate soap bubble. The world of golf had never seen anything like this guy. Tiger Woods was for real.

Living Legend

Jack Nicklaus, The Masters

Most sports figures who have reached legendary status are no longer walking the earth. Death seems to convey an extra measure of respect and charisma, so to be considered a legend while still alive is rare indeed. To reach that kind of adulation, one has to excel to the point of being almost otherworldly, and indeed only a handful of luminaries have earned this distinction. Sure, we all look up to some of the best players in their respective sports. And of course we all would love to have their talent and determination. But to really be considered a living legend, one has to be the greatest of the great; to have separated oneself from the field by a wide margin; to be placed in that wing of the Hall of Fame that is dedicated to the once-in-a-generation athlete. Well, in golf it's Jack Nicklaus. And to bolster the case, allow me to present the fantastic story of the 1986 Masters.

As the Golden Bear entered Augusta in 1986, he was already a five-time Masters Champion and had seventeen majors under his belt. But now, at the age of forty-six, the consensus was that the Nicklaus era was over. And by most accounts this claim was not hyperbole. Jack had not won a major title in a long six years and was also winless on the PGA Tour for the previous two years. So if he was going to turn back time, it just seemed that it would be fitting that it should occur at the magical Masters.

As is often the case in a fairy tale, things don't start off with rainbows and roses. Nicklaus finished his first round with a 74 to find himself looking up at the leaders. He fared slightly better with a second round of 71, but was still well off the lead. In round three he came back with a 69, leaving him five strokes behind, but still with a puncher's chance. So this leaves us at the dawning of day four.

Today, more than a quarter of a century later, many golf fans may tell you that they sensed a Nicklaus run on that final day. But truth be told, as the fourth round began back in 1986, very few media members, or fans for that matter, were giving Nicklaus much attention. But that was about to change!

Jack started off solidly enough, but when he chalked up birdie, birdie, birdie on nine, ten, and eleven, the fire was lit. This hot streak is not always a blessing, however. Some golfers actually crack when the heat gets turned up, but not our living legend. He harnessed the energy and went on to birdie number thirteen.

On the par five fifteenth, Jack reached the green in two. Sink the putt and he would have an eagle, and sure enough, his 12-footer went in. Now he was within two shots of the lead. The gallery and the millions watching on television were in a complete and utter frenzy, but not our living legend. Had sports anchor Stuart Scott from ESPN been around at the time, he might have commented that Jack was "as cool as the other side of the pillow."

The excitement grew as Nicklaus stood on the par three sixteenth. He surveyed the situation, set his feet, and deftly stroked his tee shot. Then, with the ball still in the air, he bent down to pick up his tee. And like in a moment only Hollywood could dream up, his son and caddie, Jackie, yelled to the in-flight ball, "Be right!"

To which Jack winked at his son and responded, "It is." As the ball landed on the green it spun back and just missed hitting the stick. Mr. Cool then calmly holed the putt for yet another birdie.

At this point there was clearly something magical going on, and as Jack played seventeen, everyone could feel it. With a long birdie putt ahead, the gallery came to a hush. Jack read the break, lined up his putt, and with the precision of a gifted surgeon stroked his shot ...

As the ball tracked toward the hole, it was as if time stopped. Then, like Moses raising his staff to split the Red Sea, Nicklaus hoisted his putter in the air, and as the crowd's roar rose to a near deafening level, the ball dived into the hole as though it couldn't wait to get there. Those who saw it—whether in person, on live TV, or on one of ten thousand replays—would never forget it. This image of Jack charging the hole with his putter raised still gives us chills. It has become one of the most indelible moments in the history of golf.

Jack would go on to par eighteen, finishing the back nine with a 30, which, at the time, tied the record. But now he would have to go to the clubhouse and wait. Would his effort result in a win for the ages? Or would there be a pursuing golfer who would come to ruin the party? First Seve Ballesteros found the water on fifteen to drop out of contention. Then Tom Kite had his opportunity, but when he missed three straight birdie putts his Masters dream came to an end. And if the drama wasn't high enough, here comes Greg Norman, the Great White Shark, who had caught Jack with four straight birdies and needed a birdie on eighteen to win, or at least a par to force a playoff. But in the end he pushed his approach shot to the right and missed his chance for a tie when his par putt went awry.

Jack Nicklaus had done the seemingly impossible! At the age of forty-six, he won his seventy-third and *last* PGA title, his record-setting eighteenth and *last* major championship, and his record sixth and *last* Masters. But the memory of Jack's 1986 Masters comeback triumph will surely *last* for generations to come!

About the Author

If he had been able to master his short game, Dr. Joshua Shifrin might have made a living at golf rather than earning a PhD in psychology. Nevertheless, he loves the game and is still thrilled when he manages to make a knee-knocker putt in his weekend game. Josh and his family live in New Jersey.